★ ★ ★ THE LAST ★ ★ ★
SNAKE MAN

T0386635

Snake men: John (left) and his father, George, shelter from the wind and rain while snaking at Dismal Swamp, western Victoria, in 1957. When the weather cleared they bagged 80 snakes. (Courtesy of Eric Worrell)

JOHN CANN

★ ★ ★ THE LAST ★ ★ ★

SNAKE MAN

The remarkable true-life story of an Aussie legend and a century of snake shows

with JIMMY THOMSON

ALLEN&UNWIN

SYDNEY·MELBOURNE·AUCKLAND·LONDON

Every effort has been made to trace the holders of copyright material. If you have any information concerning copyright material in this book, please contact the publishers at the address below.

First published in 2018

Copyright © John Cann 2018

All rights reserved. No part of this book may be reproduced or transmitted in any form or by any means, electronic or mechanical, including photocopying, recording or by any information storage and retrieval system, without prior permission in writing from the publisher. The Australian *Copyright Act 1968* (the Act) allows a maximum of one chapter or 10 per cent of this book, whichever is the greater, to be photocopied by any educational institution for its educational purposes provided that the educational institution (or body that administers it) has given a remuneration notice to the Copyright Agency (Australia) under the Act.

Allen & Unwin
83 Alexander Street
Crows Nest NSW 2065
Australia
Phone: (61 2) 8425 0100
Email: info@allenandunwin.com
Web: www.allenandunwin.com

Cataloguing-in-Publication details are available
from the National Library of Australia
www.trove.nla.gov.au

ISBN 978 1 76063 051 5

Index by Puddingburn
Set in 11.5/19.5 pt Utopia by Bookhouse, Sydney
Printed and bound in Australia by Griffin Press

10 9 8 7 6 5 4 3 2 1

MIX
Paper from
responsible sources
FSC
www.fsc.org **FSC® C009448**

The paper in this book is FSC® certified. FSC® promotes environmentally responsible, socially beneficial and economically viable management of the world's forests.

To my great-great-grandkids,
the ones I'll miss out on,
so you'll know where you're from

CONTENTS

CANN FAMILY TREE
(JOHN'S FATHER'S SIDE)

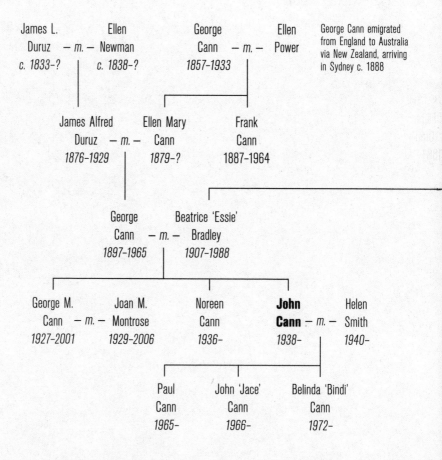

James L.
Duruz — m. — Ellen Newman
c. 1833–?   c. 1838–?

George
Cann — m. — Ellen Power
1857–1933

George Cann emigrated
from England to Australia
via New Zealand, arriving
in Sydney c. 1888

James Alfred
Duruz — m. — Ellen Mary Cann
1876–1929   1879–?

Frank
Cann
1887–1964

George
Cann — m. — Beatrice 'Essie' Bradley
1897–1965   1907–1988

George M.
Cann — m. — Joan M. Montrose
1927–2001   1929–2006

Noreen
Cann
1936–

John
Cann — m. — Helen Smith
1938–   1940–

Paul
Cann
1965–

John 'Jace'
Cann
1966–

Belinda 'Bindi'
Cann
1972–

CANN FAMILY TREE
(JOHN'S MOTHER'S SIDE)

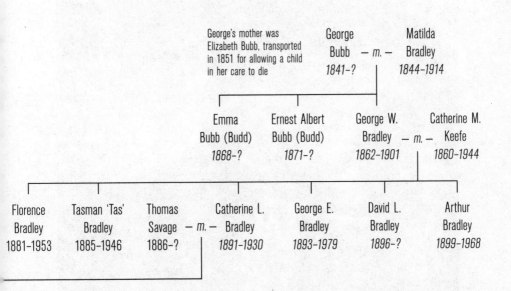

George's mother was Elizabeth Bubb, transported in 1851 for allowing a child in her care to die

George Bubb 1841–? — *m.* — Matilda Bradley 1844–1914

Emma Bubb (Budd) 1868–?

Ernest Albert Bubb (Budd) 1871–?

George W. Bradley 1862–1901 — *m.* — Catherine M. Keefe 1860–1944

Florence Bradley 1881–1953

Tasman 'Tas' Bradley 1885–1946

Thomas Savage 1886–? — *m.* — Catherine L. Bradley 1891–1930

George E. Bradley 1893–1979

David L. Bradley 1896–?

Arthur Bradley 1899–1968

George Cann

PREFACE

TO THE BIG CROWD GATHERED AT THE LA PEROUSE LOOP TO WATCH THE SNAKE show in April 2010, it might have seemed like any other Sunday. But whether they knew it or not, they were all about to witness a little bit of history.

This would be the last snake show at the La Pa Loop presented by a member of the Cann clan, the last in an almost unbroken run of nearly 100 years. In that time, nothing short of wars and epidemics, poverty and the Great Depression had kept the La Perouse snake pit closed. To all intents and purposes, through all those years, if there was crowd, there would be a snake man (or woman) with the surname Cann ready to put on a show.

Because that day I may have been the last Cann to perform at the La Perouse snake pit, but I certainly wasn't the first. My father, George, already an accomplished snake man in his early teens, started the family tradition when he came back from

World War I. My mother, Essie—once billed as Cleopatra, Queen of the Snakes—kept it going, albeit reluctantly, when he was on the road doing country shows. My brother George and I then took over after Pop passed away.

And while back in the day there might have been more vaudeville and less natural history in the snake shows, their format rarely changed. We'd bring out the lizards, water dragons and goannas for the kids to see and stroke, and some lucky member of the audience would soon find a python draped around his or her neck. Then we'd get to the serious stuff: the venomous snakes that could kill you with a bite—fatal consequences that had been proved in the past on that very spot.

Yet while the snake show might have remained pretty much a constant down at La Perouse, times did change. I've collected written reports—going back to the nineteenth century—of the early days of snake handling in Australia.

Some snake handlers think they're too smart for snakes—they're the ones who usually find out the hard way that if a snake wants you, he'll get you. In the old days, the snakeys, as they were known, would take a bite from a venomous snake to 'prove' how effective their antidote potions were. Sometimes the snakes had been milked and de-fanged (although that was no guarantee of safety), sometimes the snakeys had built up a level of resistance by taking many small bites. Maybe, just maybe, some of the antidotes actually had some effect—but probably not. The term 'snake-oil salesman' surely has its roots in these travelling showmen with their dubious wares.

I have video footage of the last public show I did at the Loop. I'd taken down my liveliest tiger snake, one that I would only show now and then because he scared me. He was too good for me, and I knew he'd get me one of these days . . . if I gave him the chance.

'I'll tell you what this tiger snake's going to do,' I told the crowd of family, friends, casual onlookers and visiting dignitaries. 'He'll wriggle, like this, he'll come halfway up, and then he'll bite me on the wrist if he can.'

And that's exactly what happened. I gripped him by the tail and lifted him. He wriggled, he came up, and he went straight for my wrist with his mouth open, but I rolled him over, and he was back in his bag before he knew it. His intent could not have been clearer. I wouldn't give him another go.

From the first red-bellied black snake I caught as a kid (earning a clip round the ear from Mum) to that show in 2010, snakes had been a huge part of my life—but they weren't my whole life. Along the way I also competed at the Olympics and played for New South Wales in the same team as some deadset legends of rugby league. I've spent six months collecting animals in the jungles of New Guinea and become a recognised authority on Australian reptiles—and especially turtles. I've been a champion boxer, a published author and even appeared in a film with Raquel Welch (well, my chest did at least).

If all that sounds so improbable for the one man that you think I'm spinning you a yarn, then read on and judge for yourself. I hope you enjoy this trip through a rich and varied life. Maybe once you start to read, it'll be you who says 'he got me!'

CHAPTER 1

THE SNAKE MAN OF LA PEROUSE

SOME PEOPLE CALL ME THE SNAKE MAN OF LA PEROUSE BUT THAT'S NOT QUITE right. That title belongs to my father, George Cann. Pop entertained and informed generations of visitors to the La Pa Loop, as it was known locally, and he combined the skills of a born showman with the expertise of a scientist. No one knew snakes better than my dad.

Pop was born in 1897, and his family goes back to the old country via New Zealand. There's a hint of scandal along the way too. His paternal grandmother, Ellen Newman, and her brother Daniel came out from Kilkenny, Ireland, as assisted migrants in 1861. Ellen married James Duruz, from Switzerland, a year later and they had eight children, the last of whom was also James, born in 1876.

Ellen's son James and my grandmother—confusingly also named Ellen (Cann)—were hooked up in what was more or less a marriage of convenience in 1897, just a couple of days before my father, Pop, was born on 16 April. Apparently they wed for no better reason than so the kid wouldn't be illegitimate. There was still quite a stigma attached to illegitimacy in those days. Queen Victoria was still on the throne, so 'Victorian values' were as strong as they'd ever be. Soon after, James went his own way and Ellen Cann kept her family name and passed it on to her son, my father, George. Ellen ended up going to New Zealand, where her other family was (and many still are), and Pop was reared by his maternal grandfather, George Cann. Pop saw his real father when he was about twelve years old. He was walking with his uncle Frank, who was about ten years older than him, and a man rode past on a horse.

'George, you see that man on that horse?' Frank said. 'Well, that's your father.' It's the only time Pop ever saw him.

They lived on the corner of Bailey (now Salisbury) and Church streets in Camperdown, where they moved when Pop was about ten years old. He and my mother never used to talk about their pasts, but I reckon it was from Frank that Pop first got interested in showing snakes. I found a newspaper cutting the other day, going back to 1908, about a strike by tram conduct-ors. (Trams figure a lot in my early life—and we were at the end of the track in La Perouse for many years—so it's maybe appropriate that the trams should provide a clue to our origins as snake handlers.)

It seems the Tram Department had got wind that some of their conductors were on the fiddle, so they'd put plain-clothes special constables on the trams to try to catch them. One conductor had been caught passing tickets that weren't paid for and he was sacked. The union got involved and demanded he be reinstated and that the use of undercover inspectors stop. Eventually all the tram drivers and conductors went on strike— abandoning trams in the middle of the main streets—and there were fights and mini-riots as the Tram Department employed retired tram drivers to get the wheels rolling again.

Inevitably that led to punch-ups, and that's where we get our first clue. One newspaper report refers to the arrest of 'Frank Cann, showman' for riotous behaviour after a fracas near the junction of Oxford and Liverpool streets. Showman? I'd heard that Frank had an interest in snakes, but this was the first reference I'd seen to him working on the shows. The strike itself— which many were worried would lead to a general strike—fizzled out after a week. The strike leaders and union organisers were sacked, as were all the workers in the power plants who'd joined them. Those were very different times.

So Frank got Pop interested in snakes, it's safe to assume. But going back to the year Pop was born, something happened out at La Perouse that would change his life and set us, his family, on a track that leads all the way to this book. Round about Christmas 1897, Professor Fox, one of the most famous snakeys of them all, started doing his show at La Perouse. Even back then, La Pa was a bit of a holiday spot for workers from the city looking for somewhere to kick back and have a swim.

It was an area of authentic bush, separated from the spread of houses in the city but accessible to large numbers of Sydney folk, especially after the tramlines were extended there and steam trams started operating. Even now it's a twenty-minute drive from the city centre, so in the days of the horse and buggy it would have taken the townsfolk a good hour or two to get there. La Perouse was also one of the last areas of Sydney where there was little or no white community. It was an Aboriginal area with its own reserve, and the Aboriginal Protection Board blocked any attempts to build a hotel or pub there.

On Sundays, travelling showmen—some of them little more than buskers—would set up their shows within the Loop around the end of the peninsula. The Loop was the end of the line, literally, for the trams, and it allowed them to turn around and head back to the city. It was as beautiful then as it is today. You have the heads opening out to the ocean, with Congwong Beach on one side and Frenchmans Beach on the other, and the bridge out to Bare Island once home to the big guns that were going to protect Sydney from invaders.

There are a lot more houses around today than there were back then, not to mention the airport to the west and, until 2014, the Kurnell oil refinery now Caltex storage—across the water to the south—but there's still a strip of bush that runs along the eastern side of Anzac Parade that would have stretched all the way down to the ocean cliffs before the NSW Golf Club built its course there in the 1920s. The Cable Station, which now houses the Laperouse Museum, was where the telegraph cable linking Australia and New Zealand first came ashore and where telegraphers were trained in the late 1800s.

The Macquarie Watchtower is still there, but the fence of our old snake pit is all that remains of the once popular funfair. You can still imagine the Loop coming to life at the weekend when the show people moved in, though. Like many a tram terminus around Sydney, it became a magnet for daytrippers desperate to get out of the city and, of course, those who were happy to provide them with entertainment and refreshment.

They had trick shooters, jugglers and traditional sideshows like puppets and minigolf. Kids would dive from the wharf into the water to catch pennies thrown by visitors before they hit the sand. A couple of likely looking Aboriginal boys would be paid to box each other for the crowd's entertainment. There were stalls selling Aboriginal art. And there were snake men.

As I detailed in my book *Snakes Alive*, there's a long and honourable tradition of snakeys in Australia, ranging from those with a naturalist's knowledge of reptiles to some who were, literally, snake-oil salesmen putting on a show just so they could sell their highly dubious potions. The first of them as I said earlier, was 'Professor' Fred Fox who, initially in a roped-off area, then later in a tent, would show his snakes and sell his 'miracle' snakebite ointment. When Fox died in India from a snakebite—a story I'll come back to later—other snakeys carried on the show on the spot where he used to pitch his tent.

Now, Pop was a real runabout as a kid, much to the distress of his grandparents, and by the time he reached the age of ten he'd roam the city alone, often ending up out at La Pa. The tramlines were extended to La Perouse in 1902, so he'd find his way out there, probably jumping on and off the running boards to get a free ride. It was while he was snooping around the bush looking for snakes that he met up with Snakey George. Yes, I know, another George; it's like they had a shortage of names back then. Anyway, the boy and the 50-year-old man struck up a friendship that caused even more trouble for Pop back home.

Snakey George was, to all intents and purposes, a hermit and looked the part, with his straggly beard and shabby clothes. He lived in a shack—little more than a humpy, really, with a tarpaulin roof weighted down with huge rocks—in thick bush at the northern end of the beach at Little Bay, near the La Perouse peninsula. George came to look forward to visits from Pop, who often stayed on weekends while they wandered the bush collecting snakes and reptiles to sell to snake showmen, museums and other educational institutions.

Snakey George would track them through the bush or find them resting, especially under sheets of tin or corrugated iron, some of which he had left around for that very purpose. As a youngster, Pop became fascinated with the capture and handling of these often deadly creatures and teamed up with Snakey George whenever he could get out there.

When Pop was twelve he caught a large red-bellied black snake in the lagoon that still exists at the northern end of what is now Pioneers Park, near St Spyridon High School. You still get red-bellied black snakes there; I know because every summer I get one or two calls to come and remove them. Anyway, when Pop took his snake home, his grandfather gave him a hard time, so Pop gathered together his belongings, including his reptiles, and ran away. With the little money he'd saved from selling snakes—Snakey George always split the proceeds from selling the specimens they caught together—Pop had enough money to buy a square canvas snake pit and start showing snakes himself at Hatte's Arcade in Newtown.

Back then, Newtown was the main shopping centre outside the city itself, and people travelled for miles to shop there, mainly because it had everything you could want within a relatively small area. Hatte's Arcade was a local landmark, and as well as clothes shops, it housed the offices of a local newspaper, a watchmaker and a billiard room.

Significantly, it also had a small picture house (film theatre) and a penny arcade, with amusements costing only one coin. It was the perfect place for a young showman to first ply his trade. It soon proved, however, a bit too close to Pop's grandparents, who lived just a few streets away, so he struck out for Melbourne, then the 'snake capital' of Australia.

Not surprisingly, young Pop was bailed up by the coppers while doing his show in Bourke Street. The newspapers were full of stories of snakeys who hadn't survived bites, and the police didn't fancy being held responsible for the death of a kid, so Pop was sent back to Sydney. He was still only twelve.

As he was clearly beyond the control of his grandfather, Pop spent a spell at Mittagong Farm Home for Boys, where lads convicted in the Children's Court were often sent. I have no idea what he was convicted of, but somebody probably decided he needed to be brought under control for his own safety. When Pop came back to Sydney, he returned to Newtown but still spent most of his weekends in the La Perouse–Botany districts. He even sold snakes on the sly to Professor Fox.

Just before the Great War, Professor Fox set off for India via what is now Jakarta, to demonstrate the effectiveness of his snakebite antidote to doctors and scientists. He left the La Pa snake pit in the care of his good friend Garnett See. Maintaining an active presence in the snake pit was the only way of holding it for future use. There were plenty of other snakeys who'd happily take over a valuable patch like that one, so it was better for him to have a friend there than to leave it to whoever might claim squatting rights.

It was an ill-fated bequest on all fronts. Garnett See came from a well-to-do family and his late uncle John had been premier of New South Wales in the early part of the century. Pop, who was only sixteen, witnessed See's one and only show at the La Pa snake pit. The first day, a brown snake got him and killed him. I found his grave three or four years ago and it's unmarked, so I suppose he must have been the black sheep of his family. The grave is about to be re-used, if it hasn't been already. There's nothing there, and it's not maintained.

A few months later, in his final demonstration in India, Professor Fox allowed himself to be bitten five times by a krait— the deadliest snake on the subcontinent. Unfortunately, it seems he only treated four of the wounds with his snakebite cure, the fifth having been obscured by blood. Despite having treated and survived krait bites earlier in the tour, he died that after- noon. Was it because he didn't treat the fifth pair of puncture wounds? Or maybe his snake oil had no potency after all, and his acquired resistance to venom was overwhelmed by too much from a different species of snake. We'll never know. In any case, a Sunday newspaper devoted a whole page to his obituary.

Snakeys are a strange fellowship. They're both rivals and supporters at the same time. When Garnett See was bitten we know he was first taken to a friend's house, en route to the hospital where he died. I reckon those friends were the two Charlie Hessells, as they were snakemen too and snakeys often gave first aid to each other when one of them was bitten.

The Hessells were a father and son team. Charlie Senior had been a bootmaker and his son had worked at the Botany paper mill before he got the boot for trying to organise a union. They lived in a tent with a wooden floor in the Congies—a strip of land joining Big and Little Congwong beaches at La Perouse. The Hessells collected snakes for the Australian Museum and other snakeys, while working their own various shows around the city.

After See's sad demise and Fox's tragic end, the Hessells took over the snake pit at La Pa and ran it on and off, sometimes with young Tom Wanless, until the war ended. Then, however, the Spanish flu struck in 1918–19, and the authorities closed all picture theatres and places of public entertainment. Face masks were made compulsory on public transport, and those infected were quarantined in camps set up around Australia to contain the virus.

It is estimated that 30 per cent of Sydney people were infected at one point, and the flu killed more than 6000 people in New South Wales alone. It also almost killed the snake shows, along with all the other attractions at La Pa. Almost, but not quite.

By the time Pop turned sixteen, he had his own tent and was accepted by most of the snake men on the show circuit that linked decent-sized towns up and down the east coast and further inland. Needing a couple of other strings to his bow, Pop also took up trick shooting and became a competent juggler. But his first great passion was snakes—a devotion that almost killed him.

In 1915, while camping at Nowra, Pop was bitten by a tiger snake he didn't see while pursuing another one into a hollow log. He passed out and was unconscious for four days before a hunter found him and took him to his hut. Pop lay there for another two weeks, his limbs paralysed, but he survived. That bite and others over the years built up the antibodies that kept him alive when many of his peers were not so lucky.

During a country agricultural show in 1917, also at Nowra, having just turned twenty, Pop enlisted in the army and sailed for Europe. The war had less than a year to run but he was seriously wounded in France and didn't return to Australia until February 1919. He immediately went to see Snakey George, who told him no one was using the La Perouse pitch. That would have been putting a fair dent in Snakey George's income stream, but Pop didn't need much additional encouragement. Still in the army, on his first Sunday back in Australia, Pop registered his claim at the Loop—and thus began the legend of the Snake Man of La Perouse.

CHAPTER 2

CLEOPATRA, QUEEN
OF THE SNAKES

THE LA PA LOOP WAS POP'S NATURAL HOME, BUT THE CROWDS ONLY CAME OUT on Sundays and takings were not the best. So he bought another tent and, leaving the snake pit in the care of two other snakeys— Rocky Vane and, later, George Atkins—took to the road again. This was where he honed his showmanship. It wasn't enough to be able to work with snakes, he also had to work the crowd, especially when snake shows attracted more than their fair share of drunks.

On one occasion a foul-mouthed blowhard was loudly pouring scorn on the dangers from snakebites, so Pop waited till he was distracted and clamped a harmless blue-tongue lizard on his hand. The drunk started screaming and flailing around, much to the entertainment of the assembled crowd.

By 1924, Pop was pursuing the snakey trade in all its glory, working the circuit around Tamworth with Ted Williams (aka

Little Sea Horse), taking bites and selling antidotes. But up in Gayndah, Queensland, they fell out over something, so Williams took the tent, leaving Pop with the snakes. Also in Gayndah, however, was the Tasmanian showman Tasman 'Tas' Bradley. Tas was hardworking and versatile, with a balancing act and juggling among his skills. But it was as an entrepreneur that he excelled.

Tas had sideshows in circuses all over eastern Australia and Tasmania—freak shows, you'd call them now. He travelled all over Africa, the Middle East and Europe, looking for new acts for his shows. He brought back Ubangi Chilliwingi, a pygmy woman from Africa; Chong Chang Fat, the Oriental Wonderworker; the Monkey Hippodrome Orchestra; the Three Hungarian Marvels, who did acrobatics and balancing; and Prince Karloy, who swallowed swords and was billed to consume billiard balls, live chickens, frogs and mice. Tas was the first to race monkeys on the backs of whippet dogs around the local racetracks, and I have photographs of him with his circus in the Flinders Ranges in South Australia with all his paraphernalia up.

Among Tas's stalls and sideshows was a snake pit. When Pop turned up with snakes and no tent, Tas asked him to work in the snake pit with his teenage niece Essie, billed as 'Cleopatra, Queen of the Snakes'. Essie Bradley was born in Hobart on 23 June 1907. Her parents were fruit pickers who were constantly on the move following the harvests, so she had little formal education in her early years (although she caught up later). When she was thirteen, Tas, her mother's brother, took her under his wing, making it all but inevitable that she'd end up working in the shows. As well as her uncle and guardian, her step-grandfather, Bill Ditchem, was also a showman, who worked archery acts and later ran a ladies' boxing troupe. As there were no snake women working the shows in Tasmania at that time, Tas imported harmless snakes from the mainland for Essie to handle, and thus Essie became known as Cleopatra, Queen of the Snakes. Later, I'd know her better as my mother.

Like Pop, Essie had a complicated family background, but her more distant family history was even more colourful. Mum's great-great-grandmother Elizabeth Bubb had been a widow, struggling to survive with her two children back in England, so when her sister died she moved in with her brother-in-law to take care of his three young children. Unfortunately it appears that times were tough and she began to use the food to feed her own children, and her sister's youngest child died of malnutrition. Elizabeth was convicted of manslaughter in England in 1850 and sentenced to 'life' in Australia.

She was allowed to bring only one child with her, so she picked her eldest son, George Bubb, who would have been about nine, and they arrived in Hobart in 1851 on the *Aurora*. He would have been my great-great-grandfather. A decade or so later, George married a woman called Matilda Bradley and took her name—probably to escape from his mother's convict name. Ironically, there are records of a Matilda Bradley arriving on a convict ship around the same time, so maybe George's adopted name wasn't as 'clean' as he thought. And, yes, there are a lot of Georges hanging off both branches of my family tree.

Pop and Essie didn't get off to the best of starts. She may have been billed as Tasmania's first snake lady, but she only handled non-venomous snakes—she wouldn't touch the dangerous ones. Pop had no problem handling venomous snakes himself, although he was always cautious around them, and when Tas offered him a job in his snake pit Pop refused to work with Essie, saying he wouldn't work with venomous snakes with a kid. Instead, he said he'd take it over, working *with* Bradley rather than for him, on his own and never with a woman. Another 'Cleopatra' had died at Manly only a few years earlier, which doubtless coloured his thinking.

So, for a while, Essie was stuck in the ticket box, but as the shows moved south, Pop softened his stance and there are photos of the two working the pits together. Pretty soon, Essie had progressed to handling venomous snakes, and with enough respect and care to ensure that not once in her career was she bitten by one.

It's probably hard to understand these days, but travelling shows and permanent arcades attracted big crowds back then. There was no TV and cinema was in its infancy, and even then it was more of a novelty than a theatrical experience. But life was hard and people needed a break from the daily grind. The sideshows and their performers provided that, and snake men and women were right up there as main attractions.

Snake women held a particular fascination, as the more daring of them also doubled as striptease artists, although I'm sure they would probably seem very tame by today's standards. My mother was not one of those snake dancers, although she would certainly have known one or two.

Pop and Mum played the Melbourne Show in 1924 and they feature on newsreel footage titled 'The Pit of Death', which I gave to the National Film and Sound Archive and can now be seen there. It is claimed that 375,000 people saw that film when it was doing the rounds. The film, which once included now-lost shots of the Tassie tigress and three cubs that were owned by Tas, also features Pop handling snakes in a manner that would scare the living daylights out of any contemporary snake handler.

From Melbourne, Tas Bradley's troupe moved to South Australia, where Pop was bitten by a brown snake during the Adelaide Show, and to Tasmania where he was called from the showground to capture a large black tiger snake that had been found on Murray Street, Hobart. On catching the snake he put its head in his mouth for half a minute—holding its jaws closed with his teeth—before placing it in a bag. This was Pop the showman, though in his private life he was much less flamboyant and in fact quite shy.

He had an extensive knowledge of snakes and could identify a specific tiger and where it was collected from a pit seething with the reptiles. He was put to the test many times by snake expert Eric Worrell, and was once handed two bags each containing a freshly caught snake. Pop shook each bag a few times and then identified the species correctly from their hiss.

At Stockton, New South Wales, in 1925, a local carnival owner, Sam Peisley, offered Pop his snake pit. Pop accepted and asked Essie to marry him, which she accepted too. Peisley then sold the couple a honeymoon tent for 10 shillings and it was set up on the beach. Once married, they broke away from Tas Bradley's troupe and decided to settle down, do their show in one place and pursue their growing interest in reptiles from a more scientific point of view. Going around the show circuit, Pop and Essie had known many, many friends die from snake-bites, nearly all of them from tiger snakes as well as two from brown snakes. So after they got married, Pop said, 'No more snake shows for you.'

The obvious place to settle was La Perouse, and in 1926 Mum and Pop found a house at Hill 60, a sandy mound in Yarra Bay (now Phillip Bay), near where Captain Phillip is believed to have stepped ashore for the first time in 1788. Pop dug a massive snake pit there, too.

There were quite a few huts on sandy Hill 60, which was about a kilometre from La Perouse. The Sunday-outing crowds were growing there again, so Pop began to show his snakes at

THE LAST SNAKE MAN

the Loop once more. He still travelled to the main annual shows, however, and was sometimes away for as long as two months at a time. He made a bit of extra cash selling specimens to other snakeys, zoos, collectors and educational institutions. When Pop put on a show he usually announced that his snakes were from Botany or La Perouse, so other showmen were always after him for replacement stock.

Mum had lost a lot of her enthusiasm for snakes, which had claimed the lives of so many of her friends and fellow performers. When Pop was away, his stand-ins were Rocky Vane and possibly George Atkins, but when there was no one else to cover, Mum still put on a show, if nothing else to hold down the spot and prevent interlopers from moving in. Otherwise she was happy that her days on the road had ended, and that for the first time in her life she had a home and could put down roots.

In 1927, Mum gave birth to my older brother, George. Life was still tough and it was about to get tougher. When the Great Depression hit Sydney in the early 1930s, the area around La Pa became shanty towns: Hill 60, and two others known as Happy Valley and Frog Hollow. Poor people from the city, kicked out of their lodgings because they were out of work and had no money, would arrive with a few sheets of tin and some cardboard, and set up home wherever they could find a reasonably flat spot. The area is all sand dunes, so digging in was no big deal, and people got on with just surviving the best they could.

The Aboriginal Reserve was one of the few in Australia that housed Kooris in the area they had originally lived—and before the shanty towns sprang up, there had been very few whites. Even so, relations between the refugees from the city and the local Aboriginal people were generally very good. It was part of Koori culture back then to share, so the locals showed their new neighbours where to find fresh water and catch fish. Ironically, during the Depression, Aboriginal people were denied any social benefits as they were not considered to be citizens.

Ever resourceful, Pop found various ways of feeding his little family. Just past Hill 60, heading towards Botany, there are Chinese market gardens, and back then the gardeners there were terrified of the tiger snakes that regularly invaded their area in search of frogs and water in the small spring creek. Towards the end of each week, Pop would patrol the gardens with two bags, one for snakes and the other for the vegetables he was given as a reward for capturing them. And in the colder months, when the snakes were a lot less active, Pop was not beyond taking his belt off and waving it around like a snake to make sure he got his usual bag of vegetables from the grateful gardeners. If they asked to see the snake, he'd say it was too dangerous: 'You saw how angry it was—he could jump out of the bag and bite you.'

In 1936 Mum and Pop moved to better lodgings in the Macquarie Watchtower at La Perouse, a fine old stone tower that at the time had extensions built around it. The extensions are gone now, destroyed years ago by fire, and it looks just like a castle on the hill. It was originally built in the 1820s, when Lachlan Macquarie was Governor, as a watchtower from which they could look out for potential invaders, smugglers and escaped convicts. Later it became the Customs Watchtower, then for a while it was La Perouse Public School—the first in Australia to accept both Aboriginal and white pupils. When Mum and Pop moved there it was known as the La Perouse Round House.

About the same time, Pop befriended a boy who was clearly fascinated by snakes and would watch the shows for hours on end and then sometimes help carry the bags of snakes back to Pop's pits. The boy was Eric Worrell, who many years later would establish the Australian Reptile Park near Gosford and be awarded an MBE for his work with wildlife and reptiles in particular.

One of Pop's show trips around this time was to Wollongong, where he was operating against his mate, the famous Rocky Vane. Rocky's skills as a spruiker seemed to be working, and he was wooing all the crowds to his tent. So Pop fell back on the old La Pa Loop method of letting people in for free then passing the hat around after the show. Before long, Pop's tent was topping the takings. 'If you hadn't done that, I was going to do it,' was all Rocky could say in grudging admiration.

Pop was also building his reputation in the scientific community and increasingly gave talks, including at Taronga Park Zoo. In May 1936, Mum had a daughter, my sister Noreen. By that time my brother George was nine years old and would travel with Pop whenever he could, collecting snakes and helping with shows. But in 1939 Pop finally took himself off the show circuit when he was offered the job of curator of reptiles at the zoo.

★   ★   ★

Before we go much further, it's worth looking at the whole issue of snakebite treatments and the development of antivenom. Effective antivenom was first developed in the 1890s by a French scientist living in Vietnam. He discovered that, in the same way that vaccines could be used to ward off diseases, small doses of venom could be given to animals—like horses and goats—and they would progressively develop immunity. Then their blood could be treated to create something that countered the effects of a snakebite on humans.

That was all well and good, but it soon became apparent that bites from different snakes required different antivenom, and injecting the wrong one could make matters worse rather than better. It was also a long and expensive process to create the antivenoms. For that reason, Pop's snake-catching skills were in high demand, as the laboratories needed as much snake venom as they could get from reliable sources.

There's no doubt that many of the snakeys had developed immunity from bites over the years and Pop was clearly among them—a clear case of 'whatever doesn't kill you makes you stronger'. But what about the lotions and potions that the snake men sold to audience members as part of their shows, as well as in pharmacies, barber shops and even tattoo parlours? Professor Fox's antidote may have actually worked to some degree had he applied it to that fifth bite from the krait. Who knows? As for Pop, it's hard to work out just how much he believed in his antidotes. In later years he would evade any questions about the small phials on a shelf in his shed or visible in photographs of the floor of his snake pit during the 1920s. But there is archive film of him performing at La Perouse in the late 1930s in which he deliberately takes a tiger snake bite and scarifies it – joins the puncture wounds with a razor cut – and then applies an antidote. No ill effects follow so we can assume he went on to pitch his antidote to the crowd.

Mum also remembered that an antidote was manufactured, and that it varied from clear to brown to purple. Pop would have her sitting for hours squeezing the juice of the local pigface plant into small containers for his mixture. The juice from this plant has been used to relieve midge bites and jellyfish stings, and a related plant contains mesembrine, a compound that has similar though weaker effects to cocaine. In Pop's case, surviving that near-fatal tiger snake bite when he was younger almost certainly did him more good than any plant extract, although we will never know how much venom that took.

The year before Pop got the job at the zoo, there was another life-changing event in the Cann family. I was born.

CHAPTER 3

WAR BABY

I WAS BORN ON 15 JANUARY 1938, THE YEAR BEFORE WORLD WAR II KICKED OFF in Europe. The family was living in the La Perouse Round House, sharing some of its extensions with a couple of other families.

While we were living there, Pop got a war service loan, and started building a house next door to where I live now in Yarra Road. That original family home was where I lived from when I was about two years old. Later on, I bought the land next door (for the princely sum of 250 pounds) and built there. Years later my sons demolished the old house and built their own places, as Pop's land was big enough for two houses. My older brother George bought the block on the other side of Pop's place and built a house there. My daughter also lives just across the road, so we're a pretty close-knit family, to this day. I've travelled all over the world, but as a family we've never strayed far from La Pa.

Pop was one of those unlucky few who had been old enough to serve in World War I and young enough to be called up for World War II. Fortunately, the director of Taronga Park Zoo wrote to the government and said he was too important to the community to be sent to war again. In any case, he'd served his country once already and been badly wounded—he didn't need to go again.

If you saw me when I was just a nipper, you wouldn't believe I would grow up to play football and compete at the Olympics. I had rickets when I was a kid—something we now know was caused by a lack of vitamin D, calcium or phosphorus in the diet—and my legs were so bowed they were almost circular. The doctors at Camperdown Children's Hospital didn't have much idea, and wanted to break my legs and reset them in the hope they'd grow straight. Thankfully, Mum wouldn't allow it and her own GP, who was way ahead of his time, said, 'He wants vitamins, vitamins, vitamins,' and prescribed sunshine, massage, and good food like meat, eggs, fruit and milk.

So Mum had to massage my legs four times a day and try to get calcium into me. In the meantime I had to wear aluminium splints all the time. They were like cricket pads with tight straps that were meant to straighten my legs, and I used to stomp around like a gladiator with his armour on. They were annoying more than painful, and they only really hurt when the straps cut into me when I was walking. But I remember going down the back of the snake pit, where our parents couldn't see, and my sister Noreen used to take them off for me so I could move my legs. I would sit down there for a while and feel terrific, and then we'd get called for lunch or dinner or whatever, and I'd have to put them back on again.

Once the splints came off permanently, they realised my legs had 'over-corrected' and I was a bit knock-kneed. But Pop said I should just run around the sandhills with the Aboriginal kids from the Mission. Between that and the vitamins, my legs straightened up, although later on I still occasionally had my knees knocking together when I sprinted. How did I get rickets? Looking back, I realise that Mum had just lived through the Depression and then we were pretty much straight into the war, so healthy food would have been in short supply. Once she got the word about vitamins, Mum used to make terrible food—tripe and kidneys, and all that sort of stuff. I hated it. She also had me eating mushrooms, and I couldn't face them for a long time after that.

I was about four years old when the Japanese sailed three midget submarines into Sydney Harbour to attack our ships and about a week later one of the motherships shelled the Eastern Suburbs from out at sea. Pop decided we were a bit too close to the ocean for comfort, but fortunately he'd made friends with property owners near Nowra. He had occasionally gone there looking for snakes—big red-bellied blacks and tigers—out in the bush. Getting rid of their snakes always made him popular, so he soon found a small property near Pyree, which he rented.

Mum and us kids moved down there until the war was over, and Pop used to come down by train to visit us when he could. My brother George worked in the dairy to pay the rent.

I was too young to go to school when we got to Pyree. Noreen got to go but I had to stay home with Mum. She was fine, but I was a bit of a tearaway even then, so I suppose we must have got on each other's nerves. I was always up to something. And it was kind of inevitable that I would get interested in snakes. Pop was an expert and my older brother George was keen. And among my earliest memories, I can recall catching my first small snake in the yard and getting a bashing for that from Mum. But I can also remember very distinctly the pit Pop had built near our house. (I wasn't allowed in the snake pit on my own when I was young—although I'd sneak in there when my parents weren't home. The pit was about 20 metres by 10 metres, with high walls, and sometimes filled with 200–300 snakes, most of which were being kept to be milked for their venom.)

Home life was very, very good. We never had a lot, but we had everything we wanted, and Mum and Pop looked after us as well as you could hope. Pop didn't have a car. He'd had a truck early in the show game, but it rolled in a bad accident, so he never drove again. That meant poor old Pop had to take trams and a ferry every day to his work at Taronga Park Zoo. And he wouldn't take the bus or tram up that hill from the wharf. He used to walk up there, through the bottom gates, through the aquarium, right to the top of the zoo. I did that walk with him a lot and it was pretty hard—he sure walked fast.

He'd work five days a week, and maybe a half-day Saturday. And he did that for years with hardly any money coming in, so he still used to make a few bucks out of the snake show at La Perouse. Life was hard on him but Pop was very good with me. He never hit me once in my life. In fact, when I was bad, Mum used to send me to my room and say, 'When your father comes home, he's gonna get you.' So I'd be in my room, and I'd hear Mum telling Dad, 'He's been playing up again,' and Dad used to pull his leather belt off and walk in and shut the door. Then he'd whisper to me, 'Start yelling.' And he'd hit the bed with the belt, and I'd go, 'Aah, aah, no more, aah,' and Mum would say, 'That'll do—you'll kill him.' And Dad would walk out, putting his belt on. But he never actually hit me. He was a great guy.

One of the many amazing things about my father was that he had no education to speak of and never went to school in his life. In later years, he started to educate himself, but when he was a kid, when he went to the war, he couldn't read much and had real trouble spelling words. Mum got a pretty good education after she joined up with her uncle Tas, so she used to help Dad. But he knew his snakes and he was quite articulate. He could speak to the public and came across really well—it was the showman in him, I suppose. And he was smart enough to be made curator of reptiles—although I think a large part of that was that he wasn't scared of the snakes like all the others.

Once he'd learned to read properly, though, he'd devour journals and magazines like *National Geographic*, and became incredibly knowledgeable.

My brother George was ten years older than me, and I was envious of him because he would sometimes do snake shows with Pop. But when I was older, I used to go snaking with Dad a lot. Every year we did major trips looking for snakes and other reptiles, and I was never happier. Later in life I'd turn down terrific opportunities that other young fellas would have given their eye teeth for—but I didn't want them if it meant I couldn't go snaking with my dad.

Life was a lot simpler back then. I know you hear that a lot, but it's true. We could play on the street for hours without a car going past. Now you'd get knocked down if you weren't across the road sharpish. This whole area, from Botany Bay on one side to the ocean on the other, was our playground, and in the school holidays we were out from dawn till dusk doing things that would give modern parents heart attacks.

For instance, I used to get an old tractor tyre, sit inside it and roll it head over heels down the other side of the hill at the end of our street. It would travel faster than any runner, and I had to be careful not to hit a light pole down near the bottom of Yarra Road, so one of my mates would be stationed there to give the tyre a nudge as I rolled past, to keep me away from it. It would finally come to a halt 200 metres across a marsh at the bottom of the road.

And I could be a bad little bugger, I have to admit. Ted the Milko used to come around with his cart and a big tank of fresh milk, kept cool with ice, and he'd draw whatever you needed into your milk can from a tap. He used to go down to the La Perouse School and give free milk to all the underprivileged families. One day, walking past when he was down at the door, I flicked the tap and let it pour. I thought I'd got away with it and he had no idea who'd done it. But two days later I was sauntering past and he came up behind me and gave me such a kick up the backside I nearly flew through the air. He knew, all right. Then there was a 'fisho'. He'd pull a four-wheeled barrow round the houses, singing out 'Fisho, fish for sale'. That was usually mainly after the mullet season, because usually they'd have that much mullet they'd give it away. You'd go down there and help them pull the nets in, take a bucket with you and they'd give you a feed. But if there wasn't quite so much, they would walk round the streets selling it.

Then there was the dunny man. Because we were a downhill run we had an outside toilet with a can for many years. When we had parties, often it would be too much and it would overflow a little bit, so all the blokes used to go down the bush because there was no back fence at the time and they would take a leak down there. But this bloody dunny bloke—whose job it was to come and collect the 'night soil'—when it was pretty full he used to tip some on the floor to make it easier to carry, which meant we had to hose it down and clean it out.

So years later, when I had my own house, I got some crap in a bucket one night and I went right down to the far end of the road and around the corner. When he went into this house to do his collection I went in there and tipped it in his truck cab and left him a note letting him know why. We had no more trouble. He wouldn't have had a clue who did it, as he was doing it to everyone else too.

Back when I was a kid, there were the clay fights down at the claypans between Big and Little Congie beaches. We'd have two sides of ten to fifteen, and each kid had a whippy stick about 2 metres long, often made from lantana branches, that they'd use to fire bullets of clay about three-quarters the size of a golf ball at each other. It was surprisingly effective over 50–100 metres. The clay was soft but it hurt when it hit you, and could leave a nasty bruise. These pitched battles would occasionally last an hour or until we ran out of ammo. It's a wonder nobody ever got their eye put out. Fights like this happened all over the district. The Kooris were the best at it, so we always made sure we had a couple in our team.

If we weren't firing clay at each other, we were pinging it at trams or passing cars from the cover of bushes. Cars were still a bit of a luxury back then, so the drivers would hear the thunk of the clay, screech to a stop, see it splattered on the door or window and then catch sight of us giggling in the bushes. Some of them would chase us, but we were too fast and smart for them. I was sorry when Randwick Council allowed sand miners into the area, as they removed the clay pits too. The clay was white with red patches, and I'll lay odds that the area's Aboriginal inhabitants in the past used it for decoration for ceremonies. It was a shame—they were the only clay pits in the area.

We all had chores in our family, just to help out, and mine was to cut the grass using a push mower. I tried to do it as quickly as possible—so I could get back to running around with my mates—but when I ran with the mower, the front of it would jump up and the grass wouldn't getting cut at all. So I put a half-bag of sand on top to keep it down. Looking back, that's probably where I got my sprinters legs from. And years later, when I built my own house there with my snake pits down the back, I would never walk on that strip of grass, I always ran.

Life as a kid was mostly innocent fun with the occasional punch-up thrown in, although some of it was quite dangerous. We kids used to jump on and off old Darkie's coal truck as he went around the streets. One time, however, I ended up with my bare foot under one of the wheels and someone carted me off to Prince Henry Hospital.

This was around lunchtime, but no one told the oldies what had happened, and it was only when my brother George went looking for me that they found out. Lying in the hospital, I knew Dad was coming because I could hear his boots squeaking—he only ever wore polished boots and they squeaked on the shiny floors. Luckily I had no broken bones—just a slightly flattened foot that was fixed by two nights in the cot.

Even more dangerous, we used to jump on the running boards of the trams and, when they slowed down at the Loop, work our way round the outside of the doors by holding bars, and jump off before they speeded up again. There were always a few scrapes from that, although one boy, Darcy Dixon, lost a foot when he slipped under the wheels. Another, Billy Hampton, was killed when he got hit by another tram coming the other way. We stopped for no more than a week after that before we were back at it again.

It could be dangerous in other ways too. I remember my brother George had taken up dancing, and I found his dance pumps and thought they would go well on the trams. Sure enough, they were ideal, as light as feathers and perfect for the acrobatics involved in mounting and dismounting from a moving vehicle. Of course, their soft leather was scuffed and scratched by the gravel on the road and the hard edges on the trams steps and running boards. I copped a few scratches and cuts myself when George found out what I had done with his best dancing shoes.

Another favourite game was to make a 'snake' from a man's necktie or a length of one-inch rope and attach it to some fishing line, just behind its 'head' in the middle of the road, then hide in a bush and wait for people to come off the trams from Sydney in the evening. When they were close enough, but not too close, we'd give our snake a wriggle and see how they reacted. At first we left rocks lying around for our victims to throw, but we kept getting hit by the ones that missed our snake. After that we'd leave a stick handy so they could try to bash the 'snake'. It was hilarious—especially the time one bloke got the fishing line tangled round his ankle and thought the snake was chasing him. We thought we were going to die laughing.

After a while if we ran out of 'customers' in our usual spot, we moved our little snake trick closer to the tram stop at Yarra. But because the cover wasn't as good, the passengers would some-times chase us. Occasionally one of them would catch us and we'd even get a boot up the backside for our pains. Happy days!

All of this came to a sudden and final halt, and it had nothing to do with the snake trick itself and everything to do with the intrusion of grim reality into our relatively carefree childhoods. One night we got chased away from the terminus, so we came back down to Yarra Road and as we came over the hill we could see floodlights around a house on a corner. This was September 1953, so I would have been fifteen years old and a bit long in the tooth for playing games anyway.

The house that was all lit up was occupied by a Norwegian war veteran, Peter Harpestad, his Australian wife Bernice and their little boy, also Peter, who was only five. I thought, 'What the bloody hell is going on here?' When we came down there and got in closer, we saw police cars. A door to the house was open and we could see a shape that turned out to be a body lying inside the side door with a sheet over it. That had to be the father. The newspaper said the next day they found the bodies of the kid and the woman in the bedroom, dead, with the woman's slip pulled up to her neck, so it was probably a sex crime. At first the police thought they had been shot, and then there was a rumour they had been killed with an axe, but newspaper reports said they had all been bashed to death with a glass lemonade bottle. The police said all the signs were Mrs Harpestad had put up a terrific fight before she was felled.

The culprit was almost certainly another Norwegian, Karl Groos, who was a friend of the family and visited there a lot. This Groos fella, a seaman, was done in by bad luck. The next day he was seen by a motorcycle policeman, near Kiama, driving a car with a flat tyre. The copper tried to tell him about the tyre but Groos took off, no doubt thinking he'd been sprung, and the motorbike cop chased after him. Then, either accidentally or deliberately, Groos drove straight into a tree and was killed. When they examined the car, the police found a blood-stained hammer and a key to the Harpestads' back door in his jacket pocket. They also found his fingerprints at the crime scene. It's pretty safe to say that if he hadn't driven into that tree he would have died in jail. It had been fourteen years since anyone had been executed in New South Wales, just up the road in Long Bay Gaol.

A woman who lived close to the Harpestads said Groos had attacked her the night before the murder but she hadn't wanted to create a fuss. The Coroner later concluded that Groos must have just gone insane—although exactly why, no one ever knew.

This kind of thing was all very new to us, so for a while everyone was wary. One night my sister Noreen wanted to go three doors down the road to a girlfriend's place and Mum said, 'You be careful.' But there was a big street light out the front and so away she went.

Once she'd gone, I went to Mum and said, 'Lend me a pair of Dad's trousers.' And when Mum and Dad had gone to bed I got the long trousers, stuffed some clothes in them to fill them out and put them under Noreen's bed. Then I got a pair of Dad's workboots and had them facing the opposite way under the bed. So Noreen comes home being nice and quiet so she doesn't wake up Mum and Dad. And she waits till she's shut the bedroom door before she puts the light on. The next thing there's an unearthly scream. My brother George and his wife Moira had their own house next door to us and George told me a few days later they heard the scream. Moira said, 'What's that?' and George said, 'Oh, that'll just be John playing his usual games.'

But it was sad about the Harpestads, and especially that little boy. I remember one window of the house had all the kid's little toys lined up on the sill. They were there for a while before they were taken away. The house has gone now. It was bulldozed down and a new house was built there. And don't ask me why, but that was the end of the snake trick too.

CHAPTER 4

UNDERWATER FOOTBALL

WHEN I WAS A KID, I WAS ALWAYS HUNTING FOR SNAKES AND LIZARDS AND the like, and I was always on the go. In my early teens I was always in the water, spearfishing. These were the days before surfing really took off here. We used to do a bit of bodysurfing, but spearfishing was the thing. It was good fun and you got a feed at the end of it, so sometimes I would spearfish seven days a week, every afternoon or all weekend for hours and hours, when the weather and water conditions were okay. We never wore rubber suits in summer, but in winter we would wear a football jumper to protect us from the cold water. It's something I kept up until I was in my early 70s.

I love mullet. It's one of my favourite fish and we used to spear a few, but they only tend to come around at Easter. We used to get a few stragglers heading north around Anzac Day. We never really worried about them, because as I said, when the mullet season was on we used to help the fishermen to pull the nets in and walk away with big buckets full of fish. They banned fishing with nets in Botany Bay for a while but the Aboriginals now have permission from New South Wales Fisheries when the mullet run, and only on weekdays. There's plenty to go around, and they give it away to the La Pa locals.

I used to go spearfishing down the coast at Wreck Bay, just south of Jervis Bay—and my sons and grandsons still do. Wreck Bay is an Aboriginal settlement whose people also have very close connections to the Kooris of La Perouse. My wife Helen's brother Bill lived on the settlement for about 40 years as a professional fisherman for the Ardler family. Bill died a few years back and the locals gave him the great honour of being buried in their own cemetery. He was only the second 'gub' (whitefella) to be buried there.

(A few years ago they were catching tonnes and tonnes and tonnes of mullet, and some outfit brought freezer trucks over from Canberra. They bought all the mullet, but all they wanted was the roe, and they would toss the rest of the fish on a tip. I like a bit of roe myself, but that was criminal. They could have given the fish to poor people or hospitals. Instead they threw them on the tip. Disgusting!)

While we're on the subject of water, we pretty much invented underwater football. I would have been about twelve years old, I suppose, so we're talking about 1950. Out on the point out here, in Botany Bay, there's an inlet to what was Bunnerong Power

Station. It's all gone now but for a couple of relics, but when it was at its peak it was the most productive power station in the southern hemisphere, supplying electricity for about a third of New South Wales.

Bunnerong was a coal-fired, steam-turbine power station, which meant it needed a lot of cold water coming in, and that meant there was warm water going out. The inlet, which is mostly blocked off with big rocks now, comes straight off Botany Bay and, with its big platform and high concrete walls, looks like a submarine pen from a James Bond film or a war movie. And to be fair, a lot of locals who weren't around before Bunnerong was demolished back in the 1980s think that's what it was.

The reality is a lot less glamorous. It's shallow these days, as the sand structure of the bay has been changed by the container wharf. But when the tide was high back then, the water would have been close to 5 metres deep during big Christmas tides. On low tide it would drop down to about 1.5 metres. So me and all the other kids would get a rock, which would be our football, and it would weigh us down so we could run or, more accurately, bounce along the bottom between breaths. We had teams of probably six or seven on each side, and we had markers where you had to get that ball past.

The length of the pen would have been 20–25 metres. You couldn't move very fast but it used to be horrific: blokes trying to take the ball off the others, bashing, tackling; and other blokes diving down to relieve the ball carrier so he could take a break or pass the rock. A big mob of us used to come out. We had no trouble getting kids because there were so many people at Hill 60 and Frog Hollow and around the Mission. Sometimes there were too many and we had to pick teams.

The outlet was a different story—the water coming out was warm and the legendary swimming coach Tom Penny discovered the channels were perfect for year-round training—there were few indoor training pools back then. Not only was the water warmer, but it had a steady flow that ran at between 3 and 5 kilometres an hour for the swimmers to work against—like a treadmill for swimmers. Tom Penny trained Barry Darke—who smashed all sorts of Australian swimming records but retired before he could compete at the 1956 Olympics—and his Olympic gold medallist teammate John Devitt.

It was about 2 metres deep upstream, and the current would take us to the ocean end. There were no swim fins in those days, so we had ropes that we'd use to pull ourselves out of the water, then run back to the top and dive in again. That warm water seemed to encourage oysters—some swimmers wore light shoes to protect their feet—so we could go down and get a few now and then. I never got any pearls, but brother George got a cheapie. We did hear of the old blokes getting some, but we were told they were low-grade.

You hear a lot these days that modern kids spend too much time stuck in front of computer screens or tapping away on their phones. A few years ago it was TV that was supposedly destroying the youth of the day. I reckon that's all a bit exaggerated, but, having said that, there were a lot of natural athletes running around the sand dunes and swimming in the waters around La Pa. And some of us were a decent size, too, which led to me being the captain of a title-winning Aussie Rules football team.

One day when I was about fifteen, a local man, a Mr Chadwick, who had a big garage in Kensington, pulled up in a big Daimler limousine with two Victorian brothers by the name of McMahon and asked us if we ever played VFL. We said, 'What's that?' The clue to our ignorance lay in the initials for the Victorian Football League. This was an alien game to us, and was widely derided in rugby league country as 'aerial ping-pong' but also known as Aussie Rules.

Anyway, these blokes asked us if we'd like to play a game, and when we said we would they said we'd need to put a team together. I said, 'Yeah, I'll sort it out.' I wasn't the spokesman, but I knew there were plenty of kids around for me to recruit. He said, 'Okay then, we'll play next week. We'll give you a game.'

So they put some posts up on a flat area that used to be a cricket pitch, down at the bottom of the hill we used to come down in the tractor tyre, and they brought out their best team from Redfern or thereabouts. Most of our blokes didn't even know what Aussie Rules was—just catch the ball and kick it between the posts was all we knew to do. But we beat them. It wasn't by much—38–26—but the other mob were pretty impressed with that, so the next thing we knew we were in the local Aussie Rules competition.

Now I had to round up eighteen players every week and get them on a tram to wherever we were playing. Sometimes I had a squad of twenty, others I only had fifteen, but I knew a lot of reliable blokes so we could always could put a team out. I'd go to their place and say, 'You go and get so and so, and you round up the blokes on the Hill.' It was amazing. We went through the competition undefeated and I have a record of every game we played—some of them we won by more than 200 to nil.

The man who was looking after us, the bloke with the big garage at Kingsford, promised us that whenever we scored 200 to nil he'd buy us a big milkshake. So we played hard and won the grand final. I was picked to go into the state side for a game against Queensland and I was told they'd already pencilled me in as captain. But the headmaster of the school, Mr Dutton, wouldn't give me time off to go up there as it wasn't an official sport at our school, so I missed out on that. He must have felt guilty, though, because when I left school he gave me 10 shillings!

And that was the end of my short but spectacular career in Aussie Rules. The next year we gave it away. We all went back to rugby league and a couple of the fellas went on to play first grade and Group 9. Kevin Longbottom became a star for Souths, and Dougie Russell played for Tumbarumba and could have been as good as Kevin but he 'retired'. They were pretty good athletes, regardless of what code they were playing.

I wasn't real bright at school—at least, they didn't think I was—but I was a good athlete and I used to win all the La Perouse school championships for my age group. And then I went to another school at Kensington, because there wasn't much sport at La Pa and all the Kooris were giving me a bit of a bashing. I don't know why. I wasn't cheeky. I was too scared to be cheeky to them. But that's kids, I suppose. A couple ended up being good mates later on.

So I went to Kensington Public School on Doncaster Avenue, where they reckoned I was such a thickhead that they wanted to send me to a special school for backward kids. The real reason I wasn't performing was my eyesight. I couldn't see the board. However, the way they worked, if you were a thickhead, you used to sit up the front. So when they thought I was stupid I could see the board perfectly. And when the monthly exam came along, I would go really well, and they'd put me at the back of the class with the brighter kids. And then I couldn't see and I had to take a guess, and I'd get it wrong.

One time, the teacher, Mr Turnbull, said to me, 'John, I can't work you out. You're not cheating, because you're sitting up the front. And when you're up the back, you go really bad. I can't work out what's wrong with you.' I never told him I couldn't see the board. My folks got me glasses, but I wouldn't wear them.

No way I was gonna be a four-eyes! Can you imagine what the La Pa kids would have done if I had turned up with goggles on? They would have given me heaps. And I never wore them until after I got my driver's licence.

When it was time to get my licence I told my neighbour a few doors down, Tommy McKenna, who used to take George and me hunting in his big Nash car . . . a bit classy for our suburb. Tommy was a good mate and he used to chauffeur Tilly Devine, the notorious brothel madam and crime boss, when she got old and was living in Maroubra Junction. And when the Granville train disaster occurred, Tommy worked for 24 hours straight under the collapsed bridge with Joe Beecroft, the policeman who set up the Police Rescue squad. That day he told me to walk backwards and tell him when I could no longer see the number plate. Off we went to Rosebery motor registry, where I filled in the form and they told me they'd call me when they needed me. When they called out my name, Tommy stood up and said, 'That's me.' When he came back he said, to me, 'Off we go mate, my eyes are okay.' And then I did the driving test.

When I went to high school at Maroubra Junction—they wanted me because I was good at sport—they put me in 1D, going on my school records, but the next year I was in 2A, and then 3A. Okay, so I knuckled down a little bit, but the main thing was I could sit wherever I wanted to, so I sat at the front. I could learn there, because I could read the board.

Regardless of how well or badly I was performing in the classroom, I was a pretty good runner. In primary school one year I won every event at the school carnival, which I suppose is why Maroubra Junction wanted me. In 1951, they had the first ever Australian school championships and I won two state titles in my age group, under-13s, and I got picked to go to Tasmania to represent New South Wales. This was a big deal because I was probably one of the only boys in the squad who wasn't from a posh private school. They had all the training facilities—whereas I trained running around the La Perouse sandhills and probably being chased by the Koori kids. I never seemed to tire, but distance runners learn how to conserve their energy even in the 400 metres. I came back with three medals—for the 100 yards, 220 yards and the relay. And I met someone you might say was my first girlfriend—well, she was a friend and a girl.

Her name was Betty Cuthbert; we were the same age and, like me, she was a sprinter. At one point Betty held world records in every distance from sprints to 400 metres, in both yards and metric. She won three gold medals at the Melbourne Olympics in 1956 and got another in Tokyo four years later. Betty and her twin sister, Marie, used to come down from Ermington in the northern suburbs and visit relatives in Brighton-Le-Sands, just on the other side of Botany Bay, so we would occasionally link up when they caught the 303 bus and then the tram to Yarra to swim on the beach.

The national championships was probably the first time I realised I was a bit better than most blokes at this lark, and with Melbourne only five years away I decided to take athletics a bit more seriously.

CHAPTER 5

BORN TO RUN

WHEN MY OLD MATE KEITH SMITH WROTE ABOUT ME RECENTLY, HE SAID I WAS a natural athlete who enjoyed winning, and I suppose I can't deny either accusation. When I was still thirteen I went down to the E.S. Marks Field in Moore Park near the showground, which was a training ground and arena for athletics. I asked the Botany Harriers athletics club if I could get a run with them, but they said I was too young and I should come back in a couple of years. I was pretty disappointed with that, but there was another club based there, Randwick. They asked me my age too, but they gave me a run and put me in with the D-grade runners. I blitzed them. When the Botany fellas saw this they wanted me back, but I stayed with Randwick because they'd given me a shot. Later on, the two clubs combined so I ended up with Randwick–Botany anyway.

By the time I was fifteen I was doing pretty well in club events and starting to get a reputation, but I was curious to know how well I was doing compared to other countries. So I sent a letter to the British Board of Amateur Athletics with my achievements and asked how they compared with other boys my age. The honorary secretary, Jack Crump, wrote back and said that while our age groups were different and they probably shouldn't make direct comparisons, my times were 'quite exceptional and were unlikely to be bettered by anyone in your age group anywhere in the world'. For the record, comparing my times like for like with the results of the All-England School championships, which he sent over, they were (UK results in brackets): 100 yards—9.9 seconds (10.6); 220 yards—22.3 seconds (23.4); and long jump—21 feet ½ inch (20 feet 2¾ inch).

We had quite a good team. Just before the 1956 Olympics, although we only had five A-grade competitors, we still won the Sydney inter-club championships. Two of us used to do lots of events—sprints, middle-distance, pole vault, long jump, javelin, hurdles, shot-put—but the other three were top-notch in their disciplines. They included Geoff Goodacre, the former state decathlon champion and Olympic 400-metre runner, and Olympic pole vaulter Peter Denton. Inevitably, because I was doing ten events anyway, that led to me competing in the decathlon. For all that, I never had an athletics trainer in my life, except for our club's sprinting trainer.

We had a Hungarian bloke called Gabor Gero, who had been his country's national sprint champion fourteen times. Gabor had competed at the 1936 Olympics in Berlin—the famous one where Adolf Hitler was disgusted that a black American called Jesse Owens had made his so-called master race look inferior. When Gabor retired, he lobbed into Sydney and wanted to give something back to the sport. Back then there were no professional athletes—not officially, anyway—and very few professional coaches.

It's funny how achievements of the past are so easily forgotten. I was reading recently that some young bloke was the first sixteen-year-old to compete in the men's sprint final at the Australian Championships. Good on him! But he wasn't the first—I was. Back in 1954, I won the under-18s junior sprint final in Adelaide and qualified for the men's final of the 220 yards on my times.

The strange thing is that if you look this up on Google, I'm not listed in the field or the results, so I can't blame the people who thought this young fella did it first. The official results only list five runners, but I was in lane 6 and I can prove it. I have an old black-and-white photo of the finish, with well-known runners of the time crossing the line. I came last but I'm there, in the background, giving it my best shot. What's more, I recently dug up a newspaper clipping that correctly lists all the starters.

A lot has changed, and not just the record-keeping. Back then, being amateurs, we didn't have the same adherence to diet and strict training regimes as the current crop. I remember one time Gabor said I was losing too much weight. Sprinters tend to be built for power, like boxers, whereas distance runners are built like whippets for endurance. Gabor said, 'Look, John, when you go home, I'd like you to have a middy of beer and it will make you hungry and you'll want to eat.' He wasn't getting any arguments from me!

One night not long before the Olympics, a few of us, probably fifteen or so, were training down at Rushcutters Bay. I think most of us were Olympians or elite athletes to some degree, plus a couple of others probably, and we all had our own coaches there. For some reason or other I went into the change room with one of the distance runners. Before we'd started our training, there'd been a cricket match on—two police station teams playing each other. They'd had a keg of beer for the lunch and after the match, and they'd left it open. They were probably going to come and get it the next day, so we had a drink.

Pretty soon the word got out and all the blokes came in, so we locked the doors and had a party. Not just blokes: Marlene Matthews was there too. Marlene was a top sprinter, and would go on to take bronze in Melbourne in the 100- and 200-metre sprints behind the winner Betty Cuthbert. Anyway, we all got on the grog and the coaches were banging on the door, going off their brains. Someone shouted, 'Oh, piss off, we're having a party,' so all the coaches left. It was a good night.

Apart from Gabor, I never had a dedicated trainer for my other events: long jump, pole vault, shot-put or discus, even in the Olympics. I just watched what the other fellas did and tried to do it better. For instance, for the first year I was throwing the discus, I was doing it in an anticlockwise fashion. Someone pointed out I was spinning it the wrong way—it should have been clockwise—and the next year I won the state title. But Gabor got me sprinting to my peak. My 100 metres was the second fastest of all the decathlon men at the Olympics. And it was a pretty good time considering there was a strong head wind of 5 metres per second and we had faster times than seven of the open 100-metre heats—that's more than 40 runners. The sprints—100 and 200 metres—and the long jump were my main events, but unfortunately I was never picked in them for the Olympics.

Coming up to the Olympics I was busy training for the new club Randwick–Botany in numerous events, and the state selectors for the Australian championships told me there would be no Olympic trials for the decathlon. It was going to be on past performances. They were happy with my efforts in the individual events but I hadn't had one high hurdles, a long jump or one 440 yards that year. 'We don't even know what you can do,' they said.

I said I hadn't had time to do those events because I was doing all the other events for the club—the relays, the sprints and the low hurdles, in which, by the way, I became Australian champion just after the Olympics. These fellas wanted a long jump out of me, so I said, 'Okay, I haven't jumped all year,' but I went out early one morning and I rolled the cinder run-up track, and patted it all down and fixed it all up. All the other jumpers were my mates so I told them, 'I'm having first jump before you dig the cinders up.'

So I had my first jump and it was about 22 feet, which the selectors would have been happy with, but the marker said, 'John, you took off 2 feet behind the foot board.' I said: 'I know. I couldn't get my run-up right.' I'd never trained to have markers, so he told me to bring my starting point forward about 2 feet. My next jump was 24 feet 5½ inches, or 7.45 metres, and that was the best jump in Australia for eight years.

And then they said to me, 'You've got to do the high hurdles.' I'd only gone over the high hurdles once before and never trained, and that's really an event you've got to train for. So I decided to run against Keith Short, the state champion and a good mate of mine. I beat him and it was the first time he'd lost a race in New South Wales for eighteen months. My technique wasn't the best—I hit more hurdles than I cleared—and Keith was a bit of an amateur cartoonist, so he did one of me titled 'Gangway the Cann Way'. It shows me smashing my way through the hurdles rather than jumping over them. Very funny!

After I'd done the hurdles, they said I needed to get an official time in the 400 metres. 'Not today,' I said, 'I'm buggered. I'm doing everything else.' So they put me in for a meeting the next week and I did 47.8 seconds, which was two or three seconds better than my previous best ever—that's about 25 yards faster. That probably got me into the Olympics straight away.

I knew my long jump was a good distance so I prepared for that event in the Australian trials, hoping I could get a shot at it at the Olympics. It was not to be; the first jump I had, I ripped the leg muscle in my knee. It was different in those days, and thankfully no officials knew, but I was injured and couldn't do much heavy training before competing in Melbourne. It's a shame. My trial long jump distance would have won me bronze if I'd been able to compete in that event and done that distance. But I wouldn't have hit the board—I jumped better when I was sixteen years old.

If you're surprised that there was no supervision of our training or injuries, you have to remember that we were all amateurs with full-time jobs. We had to be, or we wouldn't be allowed to compete. I even got into a spot of bother when a newspaper advertisement for Admiral televisions appeared with a picture on the screen of me hurdling. Obviously it was a bodge-up from an archive picture, but the Athletics Board wanted to know if I'd received any money or payment in kind for the ad. O'Briens, the agency that produced the ad, wrote to the board and told them I'd got nothing and that the ad had been produced without my knowledge or permission.

Different times—if that happened today you'd probably have an agent on the phone demanding payment . . . and a free TV as well.

CHAPTER 6

THE GAMES

IF YOU THINK THE MEDIA TODAY IS A BIT ROUGH, I CAN TELL YOU IT'S ALWAYS been that way. Only back then there wasn't such a thing as political correctness, so they would say things that would make your hair curl. And they were just as capable of taking one small issue and turning it into something else entirely. I've already mentioned my mate Keith Smith. He put together a book that contains all my old newspaper clippings, hundreds of photographs and the life history of my family. One copy went to the National Library, one to the Bowen Library at Maroubra and the rest to family.

When I was identified as an Olympics prospect, the newspapers did the full treatment on me, with headlines that referred to me as a 'former cripple' and stories that said I wouldn't be going snake hunting any more (like that was going to happen!).

When they say don't believe everything you read in the newspapers, it's good advice.

In July 1956, something happened that would have put a
major spoke in my wheels—I got called up for my National
Service medical. Back then any young man over eighteen had
to do six months' military training and then be in the Reserves
for three years. Now, given that I was hoping to compete at
the Olympics later that year, you'd be forgiven for assuming
that I would get a triple-A rating for health and fitness. I'm
happy to serve my country, of course, but with the Olympics in
Melbourne looming and a war against Communists in Malaya
(now Malaysia) well under way, I was worried.

On the appointed date I joined a long line of young blokes
waiting to be examined by an army doctor. When he got to me,
he put the stethoscope on my chest and looked worried.

'Sorry, son,' he said, eventually. 'We can't take you.'

Now, I was worried. What was wrong with me?

'You've got an enlarged heart and flat feet,' he explained.
'You must be disappointed.'

'It's okay,' I said, relieved. 'I've got better things to do.'

And with that, I swear, he gave me a wink. Now, I've got two
theories. One, somebody somewhere had had a quiet word with
the military and they decided to let me off. Or maybe he thought
my resting heartbeat of about 50 a minute, 30 per cent below
the norm because of my training, was the sign of a problem

rather than fitness. Either way, I was free to carry on with my life . . . but I remember that wink.

And so, on Saturday 20 October 1956, I went down for the final Olympic trials in Melbourne a week or so after my decathlon tests in Sydney. Although I missed the long jump team with my knee injury, if you want to get into 'what-ifs' my trial jump of 7.45 metres was 3 centimetres further than Hugh Jack's winning jump in the Olympic trials. As there was no official trial for the decathlon, I managed to conceal my injury for the rest of the day (and for weeks thereafter) and then had to sit and wait for the team to be announced.

They did it there and then on the last day, and even though I was pretty sure I was a good chance, I was a bit nervous waiting for them to read out the names. They couldn't have made it harder for me. Alphabetically, 'D' for decathlon is right up there, and 'C' for Cann is too. But no, the decathlon team was named last, and the final name of the chosen three they read out was mine.

We were measured for our Australian team uniforms the following day and there was a young lady there helping out called Ann Tanner. She was the daughter of Sir Edgar Tanner, secretary-general of the Australian Olympic Federation, and her brother Ted would go on to be a member of the Victorian Government, so you could say she was well connected. I suppose Ann and I kind of clicked and our friendship came in handy later on, when the Games got going.

Back in Sydney, my family and mates were cock-a-hoop that I had been selected, but the celebrations came to a shuddering halt when the management of Prince Henry Hospital at Little Bay—where I was working in the laundry—said I couldn't have time off to go down to the Games, which were scheduled to run from 22 November to 8 December. I was shocked and disappointed, but this didn't sit well with the other workers at the hospital who had been following my progress in the papers.

I don't know who said what to whom, but probably my immediate boss Desi Walker got involved. He was a good bloke, and used to help me train during lunchbreaks, returning the shot-put or javelin after I'd thrown them. Whatever happened, the upshot was that management backed down, although they insisted that I had to come back to Sydney as soon as the decathlon was done. It was scheduled for the Thursday and Friday of the second week, so I would miss half the Games and the closing ceremony. But hey, it was better than nothing.

In the second week in November we were all bussed down to the Olympic Village in Heidelberg, which was just amazing. I'd never seen anything like it in my life. I expected dormitories but we all had our own little houses, and I was in with the other two decathlon men, just the three of us: me, Pat Leane and Ian Bruce. There was nothing like the security you see these days, so it was very relaxed. That said, the women had their own section with a big barbed-wire fence around it to keep the men out. Not that I was very worried about chasing girls.

It was a great time. My brother had come down to watch the Olympics, as had a mate of mine. I'd give George my blazer and my mate my hat or a badge, and they'd just walk in, say g'day to the guards and they'd let them in there. Different countries had their own villages, and we could go to any restaurant we wanted to—me, my brother and my mate, wearing different bits of my uniform—and have a good meal from different cuisines.

There was a big scandal at the 1964 Olympics when Dawn Fraser was accused of stealing an Olympic flag from outside Emperor Hirohito's Palace in Tokyo. What most people don't know is that three flags were stolen at the Melbourne Games. I know because I 'souvenired' all of them—the American, Russian and a Union Jack, to complete the set.

To put you in the picture, there was a huge training ground in the middle of the Olympic villages and every country had a flagpole near the entrance where their national flag would be flown. Now when I say security was slack around the villages, the one major exception was the Russian section. The USSR had invaded Hungary that year, and some countries had boycotted the Olympics in protest. The Russians were, it's fair to say, not the most popular competitors at the Games.

Now, being barely eighteen years old and from La Pa, I wasn't all that clued up on international politics—but I didn't mind having a bit of a joke at someone else's expense, especially if that meant taking a bully down a peg or two. I'd brought some boomerangs made by my Koori mates at the La Pa Mission to swap with other athletes as souvenirs, and I did a couple of demonstrations for the foreigners for a bit of fun. I soon noticed that the Russians left their flag flying around the clock, and I saw an opportunity for a bit of a laugh. I did a bit of a demonstration near the Russian village and dropped a couple of throws near their flagpole so I could do a sly reconnaissance to see exactly how they tied the flag cord.

Well, that was a blow. It was securely tied in a series of knots that Houdini couldn't have undone if his life had depended on it. The only way to get it off in a hurry was to cut it. So one rainy night, with a knife in my pocket, I walked close to the Russian compound then dropped into a patch of shadow and crawled across the wet grass towards the pole. As I got closer, I noticed two Russians behind a large window in the foyer, but they were deep in conversation, not looking at the flagpole, and it would have looked pretty dark from inside, where it was all lit up.

I kept crawling until I reached the flagpole, cut the rope and lowered and unclipped the flag. I stuffed the flag down my tracksuit top, crawled back out of the grassed area, stood up and, soaked to the skin, casually walked back to the Australian village. Every night there would be some sort of a party in at least one of the team houses in the Australian village—and that night it was the decathlon boys' turn. So I walked into our party with the Russian flag draped around my shoulders, much to everyone else's surprise, amusement and envy. John Landy, who would go on to become Victoria's Governor, offered to 'mind' it for me. Maybe he wanted to keep one of the team's youngest members out of trouble—he was one of sport's true gents—or maybe he wanted it for himself. And, considering what happened to Dawn Fraser eight years later, maybe he was trying to do me a favour. Whatever the case, I kept it and hid it behind the gas stove in the apartment, where it remained undiscovered until I took it home to La Perouse.

The Russians didn't fly another flag from that flagpole for the remainder of the Games. Maybe it was in protest at being robbed, maybe they thought the Hungarians had pinched it as an act of revenge, maybe they hadn't brought a spare one with them.

Another highlight was bumping into Ann Tanner again. She asked me if I would like to go with her to the Olympic swimming, saying she could get tickets. I said, 'Sure.' So we linked up with two of her other friends and she gave me the tickets to hold. I still have mine. It states 'Entrance to the Royal Box'. Next thing, we were sitting a few seats from the Duke of Edinburgh.

That was fine, but then my Australian teammates were sitting across the pool in the swimming area and it sounded like an echo chamber, I could hear them so clearly. Now, having heard a few tales about me and my snake-catching and spear-fishing escapades, they'd christened me Nature Boy. So these idiots started shouting things like, 'Having a cup of tea with the Queen?' and 'Hey, Nature Boy, what are you doing up there with royalty?'

There I was, trying to look as if I belonged in the Royal Box. The Queen wasn't there, but I was just a couple of seats away from the Duke and everybody there was looking for Nature Boy. So I told Ann to start looking too and we did, so that nobody would think it was us. She was so embarrassed—but it was funny.

If you think I wasn't taking my sport too seriously, you'd be right. At the start of the Games, my knee was gone, completely buggered, and I couldn't train properly. But nobody knew about my knee except Pat and Ian, my roommates. We didn't have a physio but even if we had I wouldn't have gone, as they would have sent me home. I'd visited the United States village a couple of times to hang out with the American athletes. I was very tanned in those days, so a lot of people thought I was Aboriginal—and throwing the odd boomerang or two would have confirmed that misconception, I suppose. Two of their three-man decathlon team were African Americans and I got on great with them.

They noticed I was injured, and despite the fact that I'd be competing against them the following week, these blokes really looked after me. To be fair, one of them was the decathlon world record holder Rafer Johnson, and he didn't even win gold. That went to his teammate, Milt Campbell. Suffice it to say, they weren't feeling unduly threatened by a rookie kid from La Perouse.

I also got on well with a couple of American high jumpers, Charlie Dumas and Vern Wilson, and they started treating my injury, putting all sorts of potions on it, warming it under a sun lamp and strapping it up—in a completely different way from Australian physios, had they even been there. They gave me the treatment for about a week or so and I had to wear long trousers to hide the strapping on my knee. But they got me as good as I could be for the event.

I was nothing if not grateful, but being an equal opportunity mischief-maker, I decided that what was good enough for the Russians was good enough for the Yanks. Now, you may not know this, but if you fly an Australian flag in public, the law says you have to take it down at night unless it's illuminated. It seems the Americans have similar regulations—or maybe they'd just heard about the disappearance of the Russian flag—because I noticed that every evening one of their team members would walk the 20 or so metres to their flagpole and lower and remove the flag. It was pretty informal; the man, dressed casually but wearing a team jacket, would walk to the flag, lower the flag, unclip it from the rope, fold it, and return to the village entrance. I also noticed that the village had a rear entrance between the accommodation units.

I swapped souvenirs with Charlie and Vern, and I scored an American Olympic baseball cap, complete with the stars and stripes insignia. I started wearing it when I was around the American village, just so the others who didn't know me would assume I was a Yank in a different sport from theirs. Then one day, dressed in non-team clothes (apart from the baseball cap), I waited until ten minutes before the usual time for the flag lowering then strode out to the flagpole and untied the rope to lower the flag. My heart was in my mouth when two United States athletes came out of the village and walked towards me, but I turned my back on them, grunted a greeting in my best Yank accent, and looked busy with the cord.

'Great job, man,' one of them said and they walked on. I folded the flag up reverently and, with all due ceremony, held it high and marched it back into the United States village . . . and all the way through, out of the rear entrance. When I got back to the Aussie village, I stored it with the Russian flag behind the gas stove. The Americans had come prepared—they had a new one flying the next day.

I also got on well with Bob Richards, who was the world pole vault champion and a member of the United States decathlon team. Bob was an ordained minister in the Church of the Brethren, and he said to me one day, 'John, I'm going to give a little talk to a church on the edge of Melbourne. You want to come for a run with us?'

And I thought, this is really not my cup of tea, but then he said a few of the gymnast girls were going. They were dolls, so I said, 'You got me!' The thing about Bob Richards is that he was a bit of a celebrity already, and by the end of the Games would be the only man ever to defend his Olympic pole vault title. He would also become the first athlete to appear on the front of a Weeties cereal box in the United States—a big deal back then, almost the equivalent of appearing on the front cover of *Time* magazine.

He made a living giving sermons as a guest preacher and doing what we would now call motivational speaking. He also got into politics later on, but we won't go there. Let's just say he did this for a living. He used to go all over the Americas and all over the world giving talks, and he expected that he would get paid, either a share of a collection or a fee agreed in advance.

On the way back from the church, I was sitting in the back of the car with a couple of girls, he was in the middle of the front seat next to the driver, who was a bloke from the church. After we got going, Bob reached around and looked at me.

'John, I give talks all over the States,' he said. 'This is my first one in Australia and you know what? They never gave me a damn dime.'

How embarrassing! I was straight behind the driver and I could see he was going red in the neck. I didn't half feel sorry for that bloke driving the car.

For the record, I've done talks in America but I've never taken money for it. I'm just grateful that they fly me over and look after me. The Yanks have taken me over there about ten times now, and it's never cost me a cent. They've also taken me to the Galápagos, and many other places, and paid my airfares and accommodation and everything. But they never give me money, and I don't want it. I'm just interested in having a good time with my mates.

Another friend I made at the Games was Martin Lauer. Another decathlete, he came fifth in the competition, representing West Germany (this was long before reunification). Martin and I were both practising at the same time, and he came over and gave me a few pointers. We hit it off from then on and we're still mates to this day. I wonder if modern athletes help and encourage each other the way we did back then. Of course, we were true amateurs and money changes everything . . . especially big money.

As for my performance, I'm not going to blame my injury, but it certainly didn't help (even if my American friends had done their best to get me fighting fit). As you probably know, the decathlon is ten events over two days: 100 metres sprint, long jump, shot-put, high jump and 400 metres on day one; then 110 metres high hurdles, discus, pole vault, javelin and 1500 metres on day two.

It was a tremendous experience in front of all those people but the pressure was immense. My teammates and I encouraged each other but the atmosphere was so tense that we hardly spoke to our rivals. It was a fantastic feeling, just listening to the crowd roaring on competitors in other events. I met Betty Cuthbert a couple of times at the Games and watched at least one of her gold medal runs from the stands, but she never came to any of our parties. Young Dawn Fraser did, though.

At one point I was in fourth place on points, but that was because I was mostly doing my best events first. If I could have succeeded in getting my best long jump in, my best hurdles and my best 400 metres, I would probably have finished fourth or fifth. But 'what if' counts for nothing in a sporting contest—you bomb out on the day and you're done. As it happened, the Australian team came ninth, tenth and eleventh—with me in the middle. But every competitor had their physical challenges and injuries on the day, so I'm not using my injury as an excuse.

And that was it for my Olympic Games. I honoured my commitment to my bosses to go back to work as soon as my competition was finished, and the next day I was back on the bus and heading for home. Okay, they weren't to know what a big deal the closing ceremony would be that year—nobody did. Three days before it was all over, a Chinese Australian kid called John Ian Wing had written to the organisers and said wouldn't it be great if, at the end of the Games, all the athletes marched together, not in countries or even sports, but just as friends. This hadn't been part of the plan and he never heard back (partly because he hadn't put his address on the letter). He thought they'd ignored his suggestion, but the organisers went for it, even though they only had a couple of days to change all their arrangements.

History records that for the first time ever, all the athletes marched into the closing ceremony as a group, and as a result the Melbourne Olympics were christened the Friendly Games.

I missed all the partying when the athletes could relax after months if not years of hard training and top-level competition, and I missed the history-making closing ceremony that has been the model for every Games ever since.

I was already back in Sydney and that hurt. People would ask me what the closing ceremony was like, and I'd say, 'Terrific, oh yeah, super-duper.' But I just felt embarrassed. I had to get back to bloody work at Prince Henry Hospital.

There were compensations about working there, though. It was round about this time that I started noticing a real good-looking sort walking past, and I asked my boss who she was.

'Are you taking the piss?' he said. 'She lives across the road from you.'

She did, but I'd never noticed her. I knew there was a heap of girls living there, about eight sisters, but I just hung out with my own mob and didn't pay much attention. A few years later, the 'good-looking sort' would become my wife, Helen.

Shortly after the Olympics, I left the hospital laundry to work on a shut-down at Kurnell. (A shut-down is when they close an oil refinery for servicing. They want to get it back up and running as soon as possible, so you can make big money if you are prepared to work the hours which were long but well paid.) So I should have ditched my job earlier and gone to that closing ceremony!

Even though I only came tenth in Melbourne, I didn't realise that the 1956 Olympics would represent the high point of my athletics career. By rights, I should have gone from strength to strength and been competing at the highest level for the next ten years or more. But bureaucracy and downright racism—not to mention snaking—were about to get in the way of all that.

CHAPTER 7

RACE RELATIONS

I WENT BACK TO COMPETING AT A CLUB LEVEL FOR THE NEXT YEAR OR SO, breaking the national record in the 1-mile sprint medley relay in the New South Wales team—Bill Butchart (880 yards), Kevin Gosper (440 yards), and Gary Bromhead and me (220 yards)—and winning the national title in the 220-yard hurdles. I also found I had a bit of ability as a distance runner—as well as discovering the value of conserving your energy. Every year Randwick would stage a 5-mile cross-country race at Centennial Park. My brother George was always in it, and in 1957 he persuaded me to take part.

It was a handicap race, and being more of a sprinter, I went with the early starters who were all slower runners. But they were too slow and the faster runners, who had started at the back, soon overtook us. Towards the last lap, I got fed up jogging along with the plodders so I took off after the leading group and pipped the race leader right on the finish line. I had a pretty good sprint finish and he was spent—but I wasn't even slightly tired out at the end.

After the Olympics, and having run 47.8 seconds for the 440 yards, Gabor offered to pay me 19 pounds a week to train full time with him, but the deal was if I ever travelled anywhere, including overseas, I would have to convince whoever was organising the tour to take him along too. Sadly, it never came to that. It would have been nice to pay him back.

I loved my athletics but I was always bumping up against the bureaucrats, partly because I liked to do things my way. I was getting a lot of invitations to compete in different places but the athletics officials thought they should be able to tell me where to go and what to do. What could they do if you didn't follow their orders? Well, they had bloody sneaky ways of getting back at you, as I discovered.

There was the time I broke a state record by completing a decathlon in four and a half hours, instead of the regulation two days. The New South Wales Athletics Association bosses had wanted me to go to Lithgow but I had a mate from Tamworth, Mike Moroney, a long jumper who went to the Olympics with me, and he and his mob invited me up there to compete in a sports carnival so I said yes. But then, after I committed myself to go with them, the Athletics Association ordered me to compete in Lithgow that weekend. I refused because Tamworth had asked me first, and that didn't make them very happy.

When the Tamworth Association applied to register my record for the decathlon, the Athletics Association disallowed it by saying there had been half an inch broken off the javelin, which was a lot of rot—it was an aluminium javelin, not wood. But that was how they did things. They couldn't fine you, because we were all amateurs, so they got at you in different ways.

The last straw for me was when they tried to tell me who I could and couldn't hang about with—and pulled a dirty trick on me when I told them to get nicked. I'd been having a bit of a break from track and field, doing my own thing, snaking and spearfishing and the like. But Geoff Goodacre, an athletics mate of mine, came out one day and told me there was a night-time meeting on the next week and the winners would automatically go to New Zealand to compete against the Kiwis. The events included a 220-yards hurdle, and at the time I was Australian champion. I hadn't competed for quite a few months and Jimmy McCann, who was a good friend of mine, was the current state champion. But Geoff reckoned I could beat him, even without training, because I was always pretty fit.

So Geoff put my name down for the program and out we went. I had a few Aboriginal mates from the Mission and I was helping them with a bit of training. They were natural athletes but they were too shy to compete—'shame', they called it—and I was in the habit of taking them down to the track with me to see if I could persuade them to have a go. So I entered the hurdles and I won easily. Jimmy McCann came second and

Geoff was third. I was pretty happy, sitting up in the stand, and the loudspeaker comes on, saying, 'John Cann, can you come down to the field, please? Officials want to talk to you.'

I assumed it would be about the New Zealand trip so I went down. But they said they wanted to talk to me about the company I kept.

'What do you mean?' I said.

'The people you're knocking around with out from La Perouse,' says one of them.

'That's where I live,' I said. 'They're my friends.'

'They're Aboriginals,' said one of them.

'So? There's nothing wrong with them. They're all good blokes,' I said. 'They come to the track and field with me when I'm competing, and I want them to compete too.'

'Well, you've got to change your attitude and the company you keep,' one of the officials said.

I said nothing and walked away, but they could tell I thought it was bullshit and I was biting my tongue to stop myself from saying what I really thought.

A few days later Dad came in to where I used to sleep in the old house—just the back verandah with the snake-show banners around it for a bit of privacy—carrying the daily newspaper.

'What's wrong with your knee?' he asked.

'Nothing,' I said. 'Why?

He showed me the paper. There was a story saying the Australian athletics team was taking Jim McCann to New

Zealand in my place because I had an injured knee. That was the last time I ever ran an official race in my life. I never got in touch with them again and never ran for them. At the grand old age of twenty, I retired from athletics for good.

Being a decathlete, I could turn my hand to quite a few sports, and I was even offered an athletics scholarship to the University of Phoenix, Arizona, in 1957, organised by the Trinidadian sprinter Mike Agostini. They said I could try out for the gridiron team too, if I wanted, but I knocked both offers back. I would have been paid by the university to keep the discus rings clean and keep the lines on the football field marked clearly. Not a real job, then. I'd have had to make my own way over there and we couldn't afford air tickets, so Boral Oil Refinery in Matraville offered to take me over in one of their oil tankers. I loved my sport, but as I said, the highlight of my life was going snaking with my dad, and I wouldn't be able to do that if I was living in the United States.

Gridiron wasn't the strangest sport offered to me when I was still competing. Straight after the Olympics, Geoff Goodacre got us invited to the Inverell Highland Games, which were held every year on New Year's Eve. They liked decathletes going to these country carnivals, especially me because I'd enter anything that was going. Geoff was about ten years older than me and was a seven-time Australian 440-yard hurdles champ. He'd also won bronze in the event in the 1950 Empire Games, and at one point was the New South Wales decathlon champion.

I think he finished third in the competition the year I won the state title, so he was no slouch.

Whenever we went up there, they gave us accommodation at the Inverell Hotel, and between us we would win everything so we weren't real popular with the local blokes. It didn't matter that we were there to do what we had to do. That year we'd just come off the Olympics, so this was a big deal to them, especially if they could beat us at something.

'How about having a go at one of our events and see how good you are,' one bloke said. 'Go into the sheaf-throwing competition, if you think you're that good.'

We didn't know what they were talking about. Then they showed us this pole vault bar and told us we had to throw a 9-kilogram sheaf of hay over the bar using a long pitchfork. The highest throw would win the prize.

'What do you reckon, Geoff?' I said.

'I'm not doing it, but you can do it,' he replied. 'You'll be all right with that.'

I reckoned I would but I immediately started to wonder. They had semi-pro guys who would go around the country fairs competing for the prize money. And you also have to think there's no equivalent sport that uses the muscles you need to throw a heavy object straight up in the air, so you could injure yourself, regardless of how fit you were. But I was working at Kurnell at the time, digging ditches with a long-handled shovel, so I thought I would maybe be okay. On the other hand, they were calling it the North-East Championship of Southern Queensland, so all the pros were there. 'Stuff it,' I thought. 'I'll have a go.'

I beat them all at their own game, and surprisingly they loved us, dragging us into the bar and plying us with free grog and wanting to know all about the Olympics and whatnot. There was money involved—a few pounds of a purse—but we told them we weren't interested in the money. We were strictly amateur and couldn't take a cash prize.

'Okay,' they said. 'You can have the trophy.'

It was beautiful big cup but we couldn't carry it with us so I asked one of the organisers of the whole carnival, Snowy, who was the publican at the Inverell Hotel, if he would take care of it for me.

'You mind the cup for me,' I said. 'I'll come by and pick it up later.'

Well, I got around to picking it up about twenty years later, if not more. I'd been up there chasing turtles with a mate and we went into Inverell but everything was shut except for one shop. I asked the shopkeeper if Snowy still ran the hotel.

'How come you asked for him?' he said.

'Oh, he's an old friend of mine,' I replied.

'That's a shame,' he said. 'He got buried yesterday. His son owns the hotel now. Why don't you see him, have a word to him?'

The pubs weren't open yet, it was just before 10 a.m., but the door was open so we walked in.

'Oh, you're a bit early, mate,' the barman said. 'I can't start serving you yet.' I looked at the end of the bar and there were all these trophies stacked there—mostly football cups and the like. After all those years I couldn't tell which one was mine. I didn't say a word. My mate and I just walked out and kept going, and I never ever got my trophy for being Inverell's champion sheaf-thrower.

Another brief flirtation with professional sport was when I was persuaded to take part in the Bringenbrong Gift, a race held right on the border with Victoria, on a property called Bringenbrong. This was like the Stawell Gift, a professional handicap footrace for decent prize money (although most of the cash changing hands happens with the on-course bookies). I entered under the name John Russell, just in case my reputation had reached this corner of south-west New South Wales. They asked me if I had run professionally before.

'Never,' I said, which was true.

'Can you run?' they said.

'I was pretty good when I was at school,' I answered, again honestly, although neglecting to mention my athletics medals and Olympics participation. I had to let them think I was good enough to race, but not that good. There were two sprints—75 yards and 130 yards—and my mates told me to run 'dead' in the first, to increase the betting odds. I think they gave me about a 6-yard start in the 75, but when the gun went I discovered it's hard to run slow and came in third.

They must have got suspicious of me in the heats, because for the main race, the 130 yards, they put me back on scratch. So much for tanking! I was so pumped up for the final that I broke before the gun so they put me back another yard. At this point my odds must have shot out. The gun went, I blitzed the field and finished with daylight second. As I got to the finish line, one of my mates grabbed me and said, 'Keep running,' and steered me right to the car. My mates had done a major plunge on the bookies and they wanted me out of there before people started asking questions.

'We told them you're injured and we've got to take you to the doctor,' one of them said. 'You've torn your leg bad.'

So they got all their money off the bookies and jumped in the car back to Tumbarumba. They wanted to give me my share of the cash but I wasn't interested—not for running, cheating or gambling. I don't gamble in any form. But I got a trophy and a sash, which one of the blokes went back to collect a couple of days later. That sash is now in the little local museum at Corryong, Victoria, along with a note I wrote, telling the whole story of how it got there.

Some of the Kooris I hung around with were boxers, and I tried to help them with their road work to increase their endurance and lung capacity and the like. I used to make them run holding rocks in front of them until they were scream-ing in pain—but it built up their muscle endurance like you wouldn't believe. A couple of them—Les Davidson and Willo

Longbottom—were handy fighters, and I trained with them at Kingsford Police Boys' Club occasionally, and sometimes at Woolloomooloo. We were all trying to get selected for Australia to compete in the 1958 Empire Games in Wales.

Lo and behold, it turned out I had a knack for boxing too. I won the New South Wales amateur light-heavyweight title and me, Les Davidson and Willo Longbottom all made the final eliminations for the Australian team. For my final qualifier, they brought in Tony Madigan, who was pretty much a certainty for selection, so they would have reckoned this was just a formality.

I knew Madigan was too good for me but I thought to myself, 'If I get a big one on him he's going to be in trouble.' Well, it didn't quite go to plan. He got a big one on me first and knocked me down in the first round. I got up, shook my head, and I was all right, so the fight started again. We were into it, tearing into each other, up against the ropes, punching on. Then suddenly the referee stepped in and said, 'That's it you've had enough.'

Well, the crowd nearly brought the house down. It was a big mob and all my athletic mates and everyone was there. Although he was born and raised in and around Sydney, Madigan was fighting as the Queensland champion, so that got the crowd behind me too. Apart from anything else, they could see it was going to be a good scrap, but the ref said, 'Nah, that's it.' So it was all over. When the referees say it's over, it's over—they know better.

But if my fight was disappointing, Willo's was a scandal. I can't remember the name of the bloke he fought—probably just as well—but Willo gave him a good pummelling, from the first bell to the last. I was in Willo's corner and we knew he'd won by a country mile, but when the announcer read the results, the referee raised the other bloke's hand. To his credit, the other fighter said, 'No way!' pulled his hand down and walked off to his corner.

All hell broke loose, both in the ring and in the seats, as the officials spoke to the 'winning' fighter. Eventually he came back into the centre of the ring, but when the ref raised his hand to indicate he was the winner he looked down at the ground, embarrassed and ashamed. Willo was told years later that it was because he was Aboriginal and they didn't want to send a Koori boxer to the Games. I believe it. Racism was rife in those days—much more so than now.

In fact, before the opening in Cardiff, a clause was added to the Commonwealth constitution banning discrimination on the grounds of race, colour, religion or politics. As a result, strong objections were raised when South Africa fielded an all-white team. Imagine what would have been said if they'd known how Willo was dudded.

Having said that, the boxing officials weren't all like that. They could see that Les had potential and they took him to Melbourne as part of the Olympic boxing team in 1956—even though he wasn't going to compete. He was mainly there to spar with the fighters who were taking part but they gave him a uniform and accommodation and access to all the facilities, just as if he was competing. Strangely, at the time I didn't know he was there. I never saw him around and I didn't know where the boxers trained, so I didn't find out until later.

The day after the boxing match, I went bush to Leeton, near Griffith in the Riverina, with my Aboriginal mates. I didn't find out until about four or five months later, when I came home to visit my family, that Madigan hadn't been happy with our fight being stopped. Someone had got in touch with my parents and said he wanted to give me another fight. My folks said they didn't know where I was, which was mostly true, but they didn't ever like me fighting anyway.

Madigan was a world-class fighter. He went on to win gold in Cardiff and again four years later at the Commonwealth Games in Perth. In between he won bronze in the Rome Olympics, being beaten in a dubious points decision by a young Cassius Clay—now better known as Muhammad Ali—in the light-heavyweight semi-final. Just eighteen months earlier, he'd also lost narrowly to Ali in a Golden Gloves bout in Chicago. That's boxing for you: the winner goes around the world, the loser goes to Leeton.

It was a different world back then in terms of racism, and not just in sport. I had to ask the warden's permission to visit my Aboriginal mates in the Mission when I was a kid, and you had to be out before it got dark. It was a shame, because as I said, some of the Kooris I hung around with had terrific potential as athletes. My job at the Kurnell oil refinery was in construction and my first proper job. I was sixteen at the time and I used to go by ferry. When the boat would pull into the wharf, everyone used to try to be first off, for some reason, and jumped off the ferry's roof onto the wharf. One day I was getting ready to jump and I was next to this Aboriginal bloke I didn't know that well. I looked up and he was gone.

Peter Mongta was his name, and he became a good mate of mine. He'd come from Cann River, Victoria. Pete could have been a great athlete. He could run like a tin hare and he was quite brilliant, but he was too shy. He used to come to the track with me and I would say, 'Come on, Pete. Have a run'. But it was not for him. A lot of Aboriginal people don't like pushing themselves forward like that. And then they would have had racial interference and obstacles put in their way anyway— discouragement instead of encouragement, if you like. Pete, unfortunately, died a number of years ago and I went to his funeral down at Cann River.

As I said before, I was quite tanned back then and was sometimes mistaken for Aboriginal. Often after I'd been training at Rushcutters Bay I'd get a lift to the Matraville Hotel, where my mates usually drank, have a beer and see a couple of my mates and then run the mile or two home from there. One day I walked in to where my mates were and the barmaid said, 'I'm sorry, we don't serve Aboriginals here.'

'I'm not an Aboriginal,' I said, but she shook her head. She wasn't going to serve me. I was angrier at being refused a drink than being mistaken for a Koori. That didn't bother me at all.

'Where's the manager?' I asked. 'I want a word with him.'

Brucie Reynolds, a mate of mine, said, 'Oh, that's him there in the corner having a drink with that fella.'

So I walked over to this bloke and I said, 'Your barmaid won't serve me a drink.'

'My barmaid?' he laughed. 'That's a beauty. I wish she was.'

He was just some random drunk. I looked around and everyone was laughing. I was fired up at being refused a drink, so I walked straight over to Brucie and I knocked him arse over head. We ended up being good mates but he copped it sweet that time. Then someone said the bar manager was upstairs, so I went looking for him. I didn't know who he was but he knew me and I had a go at him.

'Your barmaid won't give me a drink,' I said. 'She said I'm Aboriginal and I can't drink. What's the difference anyway?'

'Go down, John, go down straight away and I'll look after it.'

So I walked down the back stairs and around the front of the hotel. When I came back in the barmaid wasn't there and the manager was pouring me a beer.

'I want to talk to the barmaid,' I said, intending to put her straight on a few things.

'She's sacked,' he replied. He had no problem serving Kooris so he'd come straight down and fired her.

Back in the day, a lot of hotels and pubs would refuse to serve Aboriginal people, and to drink legally Kooris had to carry what the government called an Exemption Card and they called a dog tag or dog licence. Basically, it was a certificate that said the holder was no longer under the provisions of the Aboriginal Protection Act and could move around freely and go to places and do things that were otherwise off limits to them, like drinking in pubs. Those who did have a card needed to be carrying it to be allowed to have a beer, so some of them would put it on a cord around their neck, inside their shirt when they were going out. Hence the name 'dog tag'. Thankfully, it's not like that today.

To get one, you'd be inspected and interviewed by the Aborigines Welfare Board and have personal references saying you were a good upstanding citizen and all that. Most Kooris wouldn't even apply for it. It was an insult to them and their culture. As time went on, the unions got very active in all this and would blacklist pubs that refused to serve Aboriginal people—just stop delivering beer to them. In any event, it was all swept away by the referendum in 1967, when Indigenous Australians were finally given citizenship.

I wouldn't blame anyone for thinking I was a Koori. Half my mates were Aboriginal and I was pretty much part of their mob ... still am. That's why, after the Madigan fight, I went bush with my pals down to Leeton, thinking I could get away from the bullshit and bureaucracy of Australian sport. Needless to say, I was wrong.

I had one more flirtation with boxing, several years later. I'd just arrived in Tumbarumba and the local show was on. There were a few sideshows already set up but nothing like the number Pop would have seen when he and Mum were on the road. One of those that were going up was Bell's boxing tent, which I remembered from Pop's stories of his days doing the rounds of the shows right up until the Royal Easter Show in Sydney in 1948. I spotted an older bloke I took to be Roy Bell himself and sure enough, he remembered Pop well—they were drinking mates.

Sooner or later our chat got around to boxing and he was impressed with my record, so much so that he invited me to fight his champion. I don't recall his name, but years before he had been an Australian champion, although it has to be said, like all older tent boxers, he was well past his prime, with a big belly but probably a box of tricks to outfox the average challenger.

The way boxing tents work is that they line up their professional boxers of all shapes and sizes and they get locals who fancy themselves as fighters to challenge them from the crowd. Usually the locals are too drunk or hopeless, and a trained boxer can pick them off. The ring was a canvas square on the ground, and the 'ropes' were the people in the front row of the crowd, ready to push you back into the fight if you veered off in their direction. The fighters' leather gloves were the only link to real boxing.

Old Bell persuaded me to put my hand up, but the deal was for me to be beaten, as he never wanted his champ to lose a fight. All I had to do was lose and I'd get 20 quid—which was double a week's wages. After a couple of rounds, it was clear that the 'Champ' wasn't up to it, and I was starting to feel uneasy about the whole thing. I didn't want to lose to this bloke but I didn't want to hurt him either.

In between rounds, Bell was getting quite aggressive, telling me we had a deal and all that. I mumbled that I wasn't happy, so he said he would tell his fighter to manoeuvre himself to near a tent pole and I could do the rest. In the final round, first chance I got, I hit the tent pole then clutched my 'broken' hand. The 20 pounds were mine.

After the fight the local policeman came up and asked me if I'd been paid. I told him I had and he said I was the only one. He had to step in and get the money for the local lads who'd fought. Old Bell wasn't going to pay them but this was more than a week's wages for some, so the copper sorted him out. This was not uncommon in some tents—but I got my cash so I was happy.

CHAPTER 8

ROUGHING IT

THE PLACE WE WERE STAYING IN AT LEETON, WATTLE HILL, IS A POSH SUBURB now, but back then it was an Aboriginal shanty town, kind of like Hill 60 back in La Pa in the old days. My Koori mates had relatives there so I just shot through with them. My parents had bought me a car—a '49 Ford Custom ute—so that I could drive them around because neither of them drove. I probably didn't do that as much as they'd hoped, so I might have let them down a bit there. But they told me I could take it and off I went, with some of the lads in the back under the tarp.

The accommodation in the house at Wattle Hill was owned by one of my Koori mates' relatives and it was pretty basic. There might have only been a few other sticks of furniture in the house, but basically it was old beds and mattresses. It wasn't too bad. We'd just sit around and have a yarn and have a feed—when we could afford it. We used to pick fruit, beans and grapes—whatever we could to make money to buy food and basic supplies.

One day somebody said, 'Let's go get a sheep to eat.' So I jumped in my truck and all my Koori mates were on the back when we came down onto the highway and, bugger me dead, there's a sheep running along the road. So all the young Koori lads jumped off the truck and the sheep had no chance. We had our food, but we need to find somewhere to butcher it without being seen by any of the locals.

So my white mate Freddie Bartlett says he'll show us a good spot. We went out there, and there was a big sign: 'Leeton Cemetery'. 'No one's going to worry us here,' says Freddie, but the Koori lads went off their brains when they saw the sign, they were so scared. We had to go and cut the sheep up somewhere else, but we eventually got our lamb chops.

There wasn't a lot of drinking going on and no drugs, even though the marijuana trade was starting to kick in in that area. But there was always a drop of wine around. One day we went grape picking. There were four Kooris and Freddie and his wife, and we went out there picking grapes. It was a stinking hot day and they were offering us 3 pounds, 10 shillings a ton.

We picked the grapes and put them in kerosene tins and they drove along in a truck and we'd throw the tins up to them. I had a look in the truck and saw that it would take a lot of grapes to make a ton. As it was a hot day, one of the lads asked if I could get them some water to drink, so I asked the Italian boss bloke where we could get some cold water as we were all thirsty.

'Thirsty?' he said. 'I've got something better than water.'

And he took us over to this shed there where he had a big keg of wine and told us to help ourselves. Freddie and I looked at each other—we knew this wasn't going to end well. We went back to picking but one at a time our crew members kept sneaking away and getting a drink. I said to Freddie, 'I think we'll get out of here.' Freddie had a little tin shed house off Wattle Hill, so I told the others I would see them back there.

They hitchhiked back and I later on I saw them coming down the road, staggering in the heat.

'How much did you get?' I asked.

'Four pounds, one and sixpence,' they said.

We had all worked for three or four hours picking—and they'd picked longer than me and Freddie—and all they got was about four pounds between the lot of us. That was the last time we went picking grapes. I wasn't getting work and was doing it hard, so one of the local boys said, 'Why don't you have a game of football at Leeton and you might get a good job from them. They'll look after you.' I hadn't played football since C grade when I was at school, but I'd had a little bit of a run at rugby union—a reserve-grade match when I was sixteen with Randwick—so I said okay.

They said, 'Go to the Hydro Hotel on the hill and you'll see the football team bosses in there.' It was quite funny. They said

THE LAST SNAKE MAN

when you go through the front door turn to your left and on the bend there'll about six blokes there and you'll know it's them because you'll hear them talking about ducks,' because the duck shooting was on. So I walked in and I walked up and sure enough, all I could hear duck this, duck that, duck duck duck.

So I'm standing there listening to these blokes and one of them turned round and asked what I wanted.

'If you're the president of the football club here, I was just wondering about getting a game tomorrow,' I said.

'Aw, yeah. Just be down the oval at one o'clock,' he said, hardly looking at me, and turned his back and started talking about ducks again.

I reckoned that was a bit rude—he didn't even ask my name—and I thought, 'I'm not real keen on this bastard,' so I walked back down the street where I bumped into Freddie. When I told him about the rude bloke in the hotel, he said, 'Don't play for them, play for Wamoon.' This was a little village about 9 kilometres from Wattle Hill. 'We play against Leeton tomorrow,' he said. That was good enough for me.

Freddie took me out there. He didn't play with them but he knew them and introduced me. They asked if I was any good and I said I could run a bit and that I'd played a bit of C grade and the odd game of rugby union. So they said, 'Okay, we'll give you a run with the first grade to try you out. One thing,' they said, 'you reckon you can run, but you've got a hard man to mark.'

They were talking about Ross Kite who played for Australia on the wing.

'Don't let him get away from you,' they warned me, 'because you won't catch him.'

Well he didn't get away from me and I scored two tries against him. As soon as I came off the field, the Leeton president and his mate came rushing up to me.

'You were supposed to be playing with us,' he yells in my face.

'I'm playing with Wamoon,' I said and walked away from him.

And that's how I started playing rugby league.

While I was living in Leeton, I got in tow with a character who had a big influence on me. I'd managed to strain the tendons in my groin playing for Wamoon and the doctor put me in hospital for a few days. One of the Wamoon Football Club officials, Jack Renwick, came to see me. Jack was a redhead and a real top bloke. He picked me up at the hospital and took me home, where we discovered my car had two flat tyres. My Koori mates must have had fun for the two or three days I was laid up. While Jack fixed the tyres for me, he had a look around at how I was living and said maybe I should come and stay with him and his family. He had a nice little house on an acre block in Wamoon, where he lived with his wife Mary and their two kids, who were probably around ten or twelve. Jack was about twenty years older than me.

Jack was a Jack of all trades and master of the lot. Over the next few months, he taught me all the secrets of living in the bush. At one point we were living on kangaroo-tail stews and soup. Jack used to shoot a roo every time we came back from our odd jobs around the area, like pruning fruit trees, fencing and dead woolling (where you pull the fleece off dead sheep—not the most pleasant job in the world but it was worth a pound per pound). He'd skin the roo and get the meat for feeding his dogs.

In fact, there's something I'm still a little bit ashamed about today. One time, when I went back from Sydney to Leeton, I took my javelin with me.

'See if you can spear a kangaroo,' Jack said. I was on the back of his '48 Ford ute, chasing the roos and I put the javelin right into the chest of one bloody poor beast. He only went 10 yards and the javelin fell out, then he went down hard, the poor bugger, and he was dead as a doornail. I felt really sorry for him and I'd never do that again. But we cut him up and took him back to Leeton, all the same.

Jack and I used to travel around, picking up casual work where and when we could, everything from fencing to pruning fruit trees. One of the more interesting jobs we had was to do fancy pruning in the millionaire John Hunter Patterson's gardens at his homestead called Hartwood, near Conargo, between Hay and Deniliquin. It was a big place with fancy gardens where the royal family had stayed. The block around the homestead would have been 3 or 4 acres, with beautiful gardens and a big driveway leading up to the house. There was a stunning tree outside her bedroom, trimmed down by professionals over the years to look like a big wedding cake.

They had a professional gardener—a Pommie bloke who dressed in an army uniform and was very proper. He hated us but they needed us once a year to help with the pruning because the gardens were so big. We were happy because we could eat lamb or any meat we wanted straight off the paddock.

Hunter Patterson was getting on in years but he was always out on his horse, riding his property. The lady of the house was something else, though. She was the old bloke's second wife and was a lot younger than him. She obviously liked a drink but she had all the airs and graces.

'Renwick,' she said to Jack. 'Come over here, Renwick. I want to show you something.'

'Mrs Hunter Patterson, my name's Jack, or Blue if you like,' he said. 'I don't like this "Renwick" business. I don't call you "Hunter Patterson".'

'Oh, okay then,' she said. 'Come over here, Blue.'

She wanted us to trim this beautiful wedding-cake tree, which was outside her bedroom window. It had been there for about 80 years.

'The birds are driving me mad,' she said. 'They keep me awake of a morning, chirping.' So we trimmed a little bit but she said, 'No, no. Cut more.'

We couldn't cut any more without ruining the tree but she insisted, and in the end it looked like a big slice had been taken out of the cake. All the jackaroos and the jillaroos had got the word out and they were coming up from the paddocks to see what was going on. The head gardener told us we were going to be in serious trouble when the old man saw what we'd done. It was terrible but, ironically, the birds loved it. They were jumping into where we'd chopped.

So Jack went to Mrs Hunter Patterson: 'Look, it's a long weekend coming,' he said. 'Can you give us our cheque and we'll go early? Just deduct our half-day and we'll be on our way.'

So she gave us a cheque and we got out of there before the old bloke saw what we'd done to his tree. We never ever went back. The old bloke would have shot us.

Jack used to ask me to take his family to the pictures on a Thursday evening.

'Why don't you come too?' I asked.

'No, no. I've got something on,' he replied. So I would take his family to the movies every Thursday night. It was one of those outdoor cinemas where you sat in deckchairs. One night it was raining and there would be no movies on, so Jack took me aside.

'John, I'd like to tell you why you go to the movies,' he said. 'I just trust you'll keep this to yourself.

'Yeah?' I said. 'What's that, Jack?

'We're having a meeting tonight at my place,' he said. 'It's a Communist Party meeting.'

'Well, that don't worry me,' I said. 'I'm not involved in politics, but my father was a great unionist and believes in the unions, and the old gentleman next door is a real red.' That old fella was the great-grandfather of John Sutton, the South Sydney Football Club captain, but that was before they learnt what an arsehole Stalin was; at the time, everyone thought Stalin was a good bloke. I didn't want to get involved and they didn't know me so I just sat in the back room while they had a mumble about the latest news and their membership and the people that supported them but never went to meetings. It wasn't that big a deal.

After he moved away from Wamoon, Jack became the union delegate for the Liquor Trades Union and was living at Wollongong when he died. Helen and I went down to his funeral, and Helen had a black dress on with red shoes I'd never seen before.

'Red shoes?' I said. 'Where did you get them?'

'Oh, everybody's wearing them now,' she said. 'It's the fashion.'

Well, when we got to the funeral, all the women *were* wearing them. Dozens of them, all dressed in black with red shoes. Then it hit me—Communist-red shoes! It was just a fluke that Helen had dressed the part.

It was a magnificent funeral and religion never got a mention. One bloke got up to speak and what he said made sense of all the secrecy from before.

'We've had a secret for life and we promised ourselves we'd never talk about it until one of us died,' he said. 'Jack was the main printer for *The Tribune*.'

The Tribune was a communist magazine and it used to be distributed free, or sold for just a penny or something small. I never had reason to buy one, but Dad used to buy it—all the trade unionists did. In 1951 the Australian government had held a referendum to try to ban the Communist Party but it had failed. But its members weren't exactly welcome in some parts, and *The Tribune* had to be printed in secret or the police would have come and smashed up the press. They'd get warnings that the police were on their way and they'd move the press to a different town. Jack was the main man and I'd had no idea until his funeral.

He was a great guy. Out the back of his property at Wamoon he had a corn patch almost as big as my house.

'What's the corn for, Jack?' I'd say.

'I'll show you one time,' he said, and one day I got the call.

'Hey, John, come out in the kitchen,' he yelled. 'And bring the rifle out, will you?'

So out I came and looked out across the paddock and there were about six pigs walking towards us.

'That's Reberger's pigs,' he said. 'I'll tell you which one to shoot.' Reberger was a farmer on a property about a kilometre away, and it turned out that every now and then his pigs would come down to Jack's for a feed of corn. Livestock roaming around large properties taking a feed where they could find it was common practice back then.

We let the pigs have a feed first and Jack said, 'That one there. Get him.'

Boom! I got him right between the eyes and away ran Reberger's pigs . . . minus one. We dug a big hole and gutted the pig and cleaned him up a bit and then we took him down to the abattoir at Yanco. The bloke there knew what was going on and he smoked and cured it and that pig was our food for a long time. That's what the corn was for—it was pig bait.

CHAPTER 9

'THIS ONE'S DEAD . . .'

WHEN I SAID I WAS DONE WITH ATHLETICS, THAT WAS TRUE—BUT IT WASN'T quite done with me. After a month or two in Leeton, I was missing a lot of my old mates and my family, so I came back to Sydney for a visit. The Commonwealth Games team had been picked for Cardiff and I don't know who the athletes were, but Terry Gale, one of my mates who'd never beaten me, was selected for the sprint team. I was out training to keep myself fit for football, and Terry was there with four or five other blokes.

'John, have a run with them if you want to,' one of the coaches said. They were doing the 100 metres so I thought why not. It would be good to test myself, see how much speed I'd lost. Having decided these blokes were going to thrash me, I left my track top on so I'd have an excuse for getting beaten.

There I was, down on the blocks alongside Terry, bang went the gun—and I blitzed them. Terry's father was his trainer, and he went off his head at him, cursing and shouting and going crook because I beat his boy and he was the Commonwealth Games representative. Eventually I heard Terry say: 'Dad, he just beat me! That's all.' I never saw Terry again, from that day to this. He didn't place in the 100 metres in Cardiff—all the medals went to the West Indies—but he and my other mate Jim McCann got bronze in the 4 x 110 metre relay. And that really was it for me and athletics.

Early on when I was playing for Wamoon, we had a match against Tumbarumba. Afterwards Tumba offered me 250 pounds for the season plus a job as a rigger on the powerlines if I transferred to them. So I played football for Tumbarumba for two years, which is when I got noticed by the state selectors. I was getting a reputation as a fast but hard player, and in 1959 I got picked for the Riverina Group 20 team against Group 9 and I scored six tries. Then I was selected for Country against City—a traditional game that was played right up until 2017 before no-shows killed it off when clubs started withdrawing their players. The next year I was in the Riverina side again and I got picked in Country Seconds.

In one game my opposite number was Brian Carlson who'd played for and captained Australia in twelve Test matches and been overseas with the Kangaroos. He taught me a lesson about experience and street smarts.

Carlson was fast but I reckoned I was faster, so I was just looking for an opportunity to see what he really had. At one point the ball was kicked down the field and we both took off after it. I swerved around Carlson but he grabbed my shirt, slowed me down and put me off balance. Tackling the man without the ball is illegal, even in rugby league. I yelled out but Carlson just said, 'Wake up, son, this is what it's all about!'

In 1960 I was picked in the Probables versus Possibles, a trial match that has also fallen by the wayside in the modern era, which they used to select the New South Wales team. I was playing against Ken Irvine, who was two years younger than me and just starting to make a name for himself. He was built like a greyhound and had speed and acceleration to match, with a breathtaking sidestep and swerve. But I knew his times from athletics so I knew I was faster—and now it was my turn to be the old bull teaching the young bull how it's done.

Ken got the ball and raced towards me, then tried his swerve. But I caught him and, using his momentum, threw him yards over the sideline. He landed on one of the St John Ambulance men sitting on their bench on the halfway line waiting to treat any injuries. Ken needed treatment but it was the ambo who was stretchered off.

So I was picked for the three-match series against Queensland; my kids found my team picture recently and there I am alongside John Raper and Reg Gasnier—two of the 'immortals' of the game—Norm Provan, Harry Wells, Rex Mossop and Keith Barnes. That team was coached by another legend, Clive Churchill. For the record, we played three matches and lost the series 2–1. I scored a try in two of the games: one at the SCG and the other at Lang Park in Brisbane.

Round about that time, I had quite a few Sydney teams wanting to sign me up. Manly, St George and Balmain all invited me to trial with them and get paid 30 pounds a win, 20 pounds a draw and 15 pounds a loss. Considering the average wage back then was about 20 quid a week, it wasn't bad money. Even more lucrative was an offer to play in England for around 3500 pounds a season. But I had my priorities. In fact, I was selected to play for New South Wales against the French national side in 1960 but knocked it back because I wanted to go on a snake-hunting trip with Pop and Eric Worrell. I told the league bosses I couldn't play because I'd injured my leg by tripping over a dog while I was out running. Boy, didn't the newspapers hop into me when they found out the truth!

Would it have made any difference to my representative career if I'd taken these opportunities? We'll never know. Shortly after I went back to playing for Tumbarumba, something happened that by rights should have ended my life, not just my playing career.

Towards the end of my second season, I was playing in the semi-final at Wagga Wagga and was stepping in to tackle this bloke when my mate Peter Kelly accidentally tripped me and I fell down in front of the player I was aiming for. As I hit the deck, the other player put his knee into my neck and deliberately drove down hard. It was one of those things like a car crash—you see it coming in slow motion but there's nothing you can do. Next thing I know, I'm completely paralysed, face down in the dirt and my whole body from the waist up is twitching.

I'd just seen a movie with a character in it who'd broken his neck playing football or something like that. This flashed through my mind as I lay there for about a minute. Eventually they stopped the game.

'How are you?' somebody said, probably our captain–coach, Don Furner, who'd played for Queensland and Australia and later coached the Canberra Raiders.

'It's hard to move my arms,' I replied. All I could hear was the crowd shouting abuse. They hated me. Their league team is a big deal down there and they were bagging me.

'Don't you do enough training at Tumbarumba?' someone shouted.

'I'm buggered,' I said.

'Bullshit,' he replied. 'Get out in the wing and just block.'

There were no such things as replacements in those days. If a player went off you were down to twelve men, so I said okay. The same bloke who got me was running towards me all the time—he knew I was stuffed because I was holding my neck—and at one point he put his hand up to give me a palm. It was the greatest fluke of all time. I grabbed him by the wrist and his elbow, and he kept lunging while I went the other way . . . They said they could hear his elbow snap in the grandstand.

After the match they took me to Wagga Base Hospital for an X-ray and they said, 'Oh, you're all right'.

'Okay,' I said, 'but something's wrong.'

'No,' they said. 'You're all right.'

So we started back on the 110 kilometres to Tumbarumba. Halfway there was a place called Shanty Town, where we usually had beers, and everyone was patting me on the back because we won the game. Then we went all the way up the dirt road to the hotel where I was living and I was getting bounced all over the place. Next morning I couldn't get out of bed and my arms were tingling and I couldn't move. Alan Mundy—the contractor on the powerlines—came around and I told him I couldn't go to work and he said he'd see me after.

About an hour or two later there was a knock on the door and Don Furner came in. 'John,' he said, 'I've got bad news for you. Your neck's broken'.

'What do you mean?' I said.

'You've got a bad break in your neck,' he said. 'They've just rung me from Tumbarumba Hospital.'

On the Monday morning the senior doctor at Wagga had come in and reviewed all the X-rays from the weekend when they only had a skeleton staff on. And then he saw mine.

'Well, this one's dead,' he says.

'No, he isn't,' says the nurse.

'Well, where is he?' asks the doctor, because he hadn't seen me on his rounds.

'He's in Tumbarumba,' says the nurse.

'What? You're kidding!' he says and gets on the blower to Dr Matterson at Tumbarumba, half expecting to hear I hadn't made it. The local doc, who was a footy fan, phoned Don Furner.

I don't know how seriously they were taking it. Don said he'd asked the local doctor what they should do. 'Wrap him up and don't tell him till after he's played the final,' the doctor had said. But let's give him the benefit of the doubt and assume he was joking.

Don got the doctor to come and see me and then they got me up to Tumbarumba Hospital. From there they took me to Wagga in an ambulance and that's when the treatment started. They put me in a surgical collar and after a little while I was sitting up playing cards and moving around, and then they flew me to Prince Alfred Hospital in Sydney. I was coming up in a lift with an ambulance driver when the doors opened and there was David Abramovitch, a mate from athletics—he'd been a handy 440-yards runner for the Sydney University team—and was now a big-time orthopaedic surgeon.

'It's not you, is it? Your neck?' he asked.

When I said it was, he got these other two doctors he had with him and they held me by the head and walked me to a bed.

'I'm all right,' I said. 'I've been walking around for days.'

'Don't move,' he said. He'd had the X-rays sent with me and had had a look at them already. The crack in my vertebrae was right down to the spinal cord but, thankfully, no further.

About 25 years later, I went for an X-ray on my shoulders—I forget what was wrong with them—and I knew the radiologist, Luke, because he worked with my daughter, Belinda.

Luke walked in to see me. 'John, are you all right?' he said.

'Yeah, why?'

'Your neck's broken,' he said. 'There's a big crack in your neck.'

'Oh, don't worry about it,' I said. 'It's always been there.'

At Prince Alfred they wouldn't even let me lie down on the bed. They put a board against my head, and strapped me to it. Then they picked the board up and laid me on the bed, put traction under my chin then pulled the board out. It was a bastard. When I came out of traction a few weeks later they said, 'Well, that's as good as it's going to be.' Next thing they were putting me in a full-torso plaster, from my hips to the top of my head with just a hole for my face and my ears. And that was me for the next two or three months.

Tumbarumba played the grand final against Yenda the next weekend. One of the radio stations—ABC or 2UE, I can't remember which—covered the game and they played it to me in the hospital. It was a two-all draw after extra time, so they played again the next week and Tumbarumba won 8-6.

I was in hospital for a couple of months. There were about twelve people with broken necks in my ward at Prince Alfred and I was the only one who could walk. The rest of them were paralysed to different degrees. One of the poor buggers had been in a car accident and he could only use one hand. They used to let him shave himself with an electric razor until they caught him chewing the cable in an effort to electrocute himself.

I was lucky. For me, the worst thing was this itch at the back of my head that was starting to drive me off my brain. A few of the other patients were weaving baskets so I got a bit of cane off somebody and I put it through one ear hole in the plaster and I worked for maybe an hour or more to get the cane to come out the other hole. Eventually I got it out and I could scratch the back of my head. Bliss! Then I was lying there with my eyes shut and the next thing I heard was *swish* as the curtains opened and a nurse said, 'What's this doing here?' and pulled the cane out. I could have wept. It had taken me ages to get it in.

When they let me out of hospital, I went back to Sydney at first but I was so hot inside the cast that my family took me back to Tumbarumba. I had a good old mate there I used to go into the bush with. His name was Charlie Kellam and his son Barry was in my football team. He had a really cool room in his house and I used to lie there most of the time, escaping the heat.

I'd lie there all day if I could. I didn't feel like ever getting up. I just wanted to sleep, sleep, sleep. One day Charlie came in and said: 'Come on, Jack'—he used to call me Jack—'Get up. Breakfast'.

He shook me to get up then he gave out a scream. I had my pyjamas on and a blanket or a sheet over me and he'd forgotten about the plaster cast and thought I was stiff and dead. Scared the hell out of poor old Charlie.

I suppose I was lucky. After I got the plaster off, I was working the jackhammer on a building site, just wearing a neck brace. It must have looked strange but it didn't seem to bother me. But I wasn't 100 per cent. For months after that I'd be sitting there with a beer or a glass of water in my hand and the next thing I heard, *smash*, and it would be on the ground. I never even knew it was out of my hand. This kept happening—I'd just lose the feeling in my fingers.

Around that time, South Sydney wanted me to play for them and so they sent me to see their doctor. He X-rayed me and asked me how I was going, if I'd any other symptoms, that kind of thing. Then he said: 'I think you'd be right to play again.' But my other doctors told me not to even think about it.

I would never have played again except I did have one game in the bush, mainly because I owed Charlie a favour. His son, Barry, was captain–coach of the team in a little town called Boggabri and they were playing Narrabri. I was working on the powerlines up through that country and one day a Volkswagen came down the road.

'Jeez, I know that car,' I thought. Sure, enough it was my old mate Charlie.

'Come and have a game with us,' he said. 'Play for us. They'll pay you good money.'

I was working hard and I felt all right so I said okay, even though it would mean taking a day off work. It was a long drive—almost 200 kilometres on minor roads—from where I was at

Coolatai to go down to Narrabri. I went well, playing half a game in reserve grade and then another half in the firsts where I scored a try and we won.

Then we went back with the team to Boggabri, about 50 kilometres further on, and all got on the grog. It was ten o'clock at night and it was stinking hot and I had two mates from work with me. The team manager came up and said, 'Oh, John, we were pretty pleased with you. Next week we'll start paying you.' Next week? I thought I *was* getting paid, at least for the day I took off work!

When we headed back to Coolatai I decided to take the long way round on the bitumen road through Moree but got totally lost thanks to my drunk mates giving me seriously bad directions. At one point, and this was late at night, we stopped at a milk bar in Wee Waa and the owner told us we were 30 kilometres in the wrong direction and needed to go back to Narrabri. So we decided to take a shortcut and ended up on a dirt road going nowhere until we saw a car lights coming the other way. We had to stop before we got to him as the dust we were kicking up was so thick. It turned out he was lost too—but at least he could tell us where the Moree road was.

I was so tired and sore after that day that I never played football again. Months and months later, when the season was all over, Barry and I caught up with each other and he asked why I didn't play for them again.

'Me and my mates took the day off work, drove 500 kilometres and they never paid me,' I said.

'Are you fair dinkum?' he said. 'Why the friggin hell didn't you tell me?'

'What was the good of starting an argument, Barry?' I said.

You can't spend your life brooding about missed opportunities. When I got my neck broken I was seriously thinking about taking up that offer to play for a club in Sydney or even pack my bags and go and play in England where the money on offer would have made up for the cold weather. On the other hand, they only have two breeds of snake in Britain.

As for the bloke who broke my neck, like they say, what goes around comes around. I never met him again but twenty years later a Koori mate went into his butcher shop in a Sydney surbub. The bloke asked my mate where he was from and when he said La Perouse, he asked him if he knew John Cann.

'Yes, I do,' says my mate. 'Why do you ask?'

'I played football against him,' says the butcher and gives my mate his business card. 'Tell John to drop in and see me some time.'

I never went near him. I hated his guts for what he did—and what he nearly did to me. I knew damn well it was deliberate. The only upside was that he still had splints on his arm (from where I broke it trying to fend him off) long after I'd recovered, and he never played football again.

CHAPTER 10

WORK

JUST IN CASE YOU THINK MY LIFE WAS ALL FUN AND GAMES, WHILE ALL THAT was going on I was working full time almost from the day I left school at sixteen. Nowadays you would look for a job on the internet, but back then it was the bush telegraph or you went from door to door, building site to building site.

When I left school I was taken on as an apprentice fitter and turner at H.C. Sligh, a branch of the Wills tobacco factory in Kensington. As ever, athletics was a factor, as the Australian pole vault champion Peter Denton, who had a senior position in the firm, got me in there . . . but I hated it. I was working indoors on the machines and every day I said to myself 'F . . . ! What am I doing here?' I needed to be outside—not stuck in a noisy, dirty factory.

Even so, I gave it my best shot, and when I went to tech college I was getting good marks in all my exams. After my three-month test, the boss wanted me to sign up permanently. I said I wasn't sure. I needed to take some time to think about it. They said they'd give me another three months and after that they called me into the office. They had the papers all there, ready for me to sign, but I said I'd decided not to do it. The boss was furious. He ripped the papers up and threw them at me.

'Get the hell out of my office!' he yelled. 'You're done here.'

And that was the end of my career as a fitter and turner. I'd been getting five pounds, one and sixpence a week, plus a packet of cigarettes.

The following week my mates and I all went looking for jobs, the six of us together. One bloke interviewed us all, standing there together in his office, and then he sent us away. Next thing, he called me back and offered me a job—but only me. I said, 'No, thanks.' It was all six of us or nothing. Can you imagine the sheer gall of it? Believe it or not, we walked down the road towards the Kellogg's factory and there was a company there called Patricks—they hired the lot of us on the spot.

It turned out to be a short job, and that's when I went to work at the Caltex site at Kurnell, along with all my mates, digging foundations and laying concrete slabs for the new refinery. I've got a photo of me in the trenches, on the shovels with my mates, digging footings. Eric Worrell, who would later open the reptile park at Gosford, was doing an article about my athletics, found out where I was working, and came down and took the photograph.

I liked being outdoors and enjoyed the physical work—and the money was much better too, especially for a young fella living with his parents. I saved up 250 pounds and was planning to buy a motorbike. I had my eye on a Triumph Tiger 110, the kind the police used. That plan lasted just about long enough for me to tell my dad about it.

'You're not buying a motorbike,' Pop said. 'There's a plot of land for sale next to us and you're buying that.'

So that was me, a landowner before I was out of my teens. I built the house I'm sitting in now on that land—and I have to concede it was a shrewd investment. I'm lucky I didn't get the bike—I would probably have killed myself on it.

I worked on construction at Caltex while there was work, and then in the laundry at Prince Henry Hospital in the lead-up to the Olympics. Years later, ironically, I would also get occasional work at Caltex as a rigger. And then, many, many years later, after I was retired, a friend, Andrew Melrose, and I were hired by Caltex to relocate the red-bellied black snakes, which were in big numbers at Kurnell. We caught up to eight a day and moved them to a safe spot not far away.

This hunt was carried out once a week over a number of years, but it finished in 2016 when the new boss decided to cut costs—and dudded me out of two days' pay. But I imagine that was probably the longest anyone ever worked at Caltex in the world—on and off it added up to 62 years. Relocating the snakes could not have offered more of a contrast with the ecological vandalism that occurred when I worked there in my teens.

When the construction site was being levelled it was done by dredging Botany Bay to make it deeper for the tankers, and pumping millions of cubic metres of sand to fill the swamps and small lagoons. This was an environmental disaster; there were hundreds if not thousands of freshwater turtles buried alive, but nothing was ever said (although years later I think there was an article in *Australian Geographic* magazine).

Before the Olympic Games I was on a jackhammer in Sydney city, drilling holes in solid rock for the footings of big new buildings. The holes were about 4 metres deep and 1.5 metres wide by 1.8 metres long. When I filled a bucket with rock, a mate would pull the bucket up on a rope and often a rock would fall out of the bucket and nearly hit me on the head. There were no hard hats in those days, so I used to put the shovel over my head to protect myself. And all the time I was still training for athletics. To answer the obvious question: no, I didn't know what I wanted to do when I grew up . . . I still don't.

When I was about sixteen I was approached by Brucie Reynolds' dad—who was a mad-keen gambler.

'Are you interested in turning professional?' he said.

'Not really, why?' I replied

'We can guarantee you some good money,' he said. 'We want you to run in the Stawell Gift. We'll get you a big start and no one will catch you.'

I wasn't interested and knocked it back, but it figured in a very strange coincidence. A couple of years later I was working in the city, down the end of George Street, jackhammering and loading all the rubble onto the back of the trucks. It was hard but I was fit. One day I was shovelling away there and this bloke sang out to me, 'Hey, John. John Cann!'

He was at the end of a ramp up to the roadway and I looked up at him, but the light was behind him and my eyes weren't that great at the best of times, so I walked up towards him, trying to work out who he was.

'John?' he said. Then, as I got closer, 'Oh, sorry mate. You're not John Cann.'

'Yes, I am,' I said.

'Nah, you're too young,' he replied.

We chatted for a bit and it turned out he thought I was a John Cann from Broken Hill who—now get this—had won the Stawell Gift! I couldn't get over there being another John Cann out there who was a runner. Later I found a newspaper cutting with a photo of the J.E. Cann who won the Gift in 1949, eight or nine years earlier. It was a bad picture and I suppose he did look a bit like me, but what a coincidence!

In Tumbarumba I had the job on powerline construction, through a fella called Alan Munday. He had me and three Italian blokes putting powerlines through the district and down to the edge of the Snowy Mountains. I learned all the tricks of the trade down there and worked sometimes seven days a week, three weeks on and six days off.

Working in the bush allowed me to keep catching snakes to take home to Pop, and diving for freshwater turtles—a growing interest of mine—in my spare time. I stayed on the powerline construction for years, on and off.

We were basically digging monstrous big logs, about 20 metres long, into 2–3-metre deep holes, then holding them up with cables attached to trucks until the stays were in place. Then we would 'terminate' them—attach the power cables to the insulators on the cross-pieces. One time when I was foreman, three of us were up the pole terminating and there were three big army trucks, one on each cable. Everything looked right so I told the truck drivers to take the weight off because the stays were in place and the pole would hold.

It was the right tension but the weld on the stay broke and the only reason I and the other two blokes are here today is that one of the trucks had stalled and it stopped the pole from snapping or being pulled out of the ground by the tension on the power cables. I said to my mates, 'Don't move an inch.' They ignored me. They were down that pole like bullets and I followed them. There was a domino effect back down the lines and they were damaged for miles. It cost thousands of dollars to repair, but the contractor was compensated because it was a faulty weld on the stay.

I loved the work, though. I used to work hard and long, sometimes fourteen or fifteen hours a day. I never got that much money, but I was able to save enough to build my house because there was nothing to spend it on out in the bush. We got onto some big lines up in southern Queensland, where I was also working as foreman. I started to study then because the inspectors found out I was powering the lines up without being qualified. I'd been considering doing my linesman's ticket certificate anyway, but this spurred me on to do it by correspondence.

Out in the bush, often miles away from any towns, the boss used to rent properties for us, like shearing quarters or abandoned homesteads, so we always had good accommodation. Two beds and a little window. Bring your own mosquito net.

On some of the jobs we took turns at cooking, but on bigger jobs we got a cook. One time we had a terrible cook when her husband got a job with us. The place had big fuel stoves, so she used to fry the eggs at night-time so she didn't have to fire up the stove in the morning, when she just heated them up on the little fuel stove off the side. We weren't happy with her but the boss was away and how could we sack them both?

One day I caught a king brown snake more than 7 feet long and I put him in a big chaff bag. Normally with snakes we would use sugar bags or some other big smooth bag, but not chaff bags as they can push their way out—as we discovered. I put it in the grain shed at the end of the row of all the little rooms we had, and made a box up to put the big king brown in to take home to Pop. Then one day my mate Barry came out with the empty bag and said, 'He's gone.' He must have escaped under the floorboards. I made up a sign with a drawing of a snake's head with big fangs and dripping venom and the words 'Missing brown snake. Bites likes a dog. Extremely deadly!' and stuck it on the wall.

'Are you serious?' said the cook's husband. 'That snake's got away?'

When I answered yes, he and his wife packed up and went straight back to Goondiwindi where they came from. That saved us sacking the cook . . . and he was pretty useless too. Some time after that I brought in a mate of mine from Sydney, Vic Dalton, as our cook. He was a good mechanic too and he came up with his wife. He did the cooking and a bit of everything.

Later on, between jobs, Vic and I started our own business installing car-wash equipment in petrol stations from Queensland down to Tasmania. All the machinery was imported and delivered to the petrol stations. They'd have the building up and ready and we'd just unpack the boxes and install it and it was good to go.

But it was while I was working on the powerlines from Armidale over the mountains to the Macleay River that two life-changing events occurred. The first was that I was diving for turtles in my spare time when I found what I considered to be my first new species.

Meanwhile I was going out with Helen when I came back to Sydney. I'd be away three or four months at a time and then come home for a spell and then I'd be off again. Up in Armidale, I got a letter from Helen.

'I've booked our wedding on 29 February 1964,' it said. I burst out laughing.

'There's only 28 days in February,' I said to my mate.

'Next year has 29,' he said. 'It's a leap year.'

CHAPTER 11

SNAKING

YOU'VE PROBABLY REALISED BY NOW THAT ALL THE TIME I WAS GROWING UP, playing sport and working, I was fascinated by snakes. I hated it when Pop used to go snaking with my brother George but later he'd take me on a Saturday afternoon or Sunday morning. There were a lot of snakes around back then. Pop got thirteen tiger snakes one day at Eastlakes swamps and I have a photograph of him, taken for a newspaper story, taking one from high up in a tree. The most he ever got on his own in one go was 26, around the Chinese market gardens at Botany. At least once a week in the summer months we'd be called to get a tiger snake off Yarra Road or La Perouse School and once in the foyer of the Yarra Bay Sailing Club. They used to come up from the swamp at the bottom of that tyre-rolling hill. But no one was ever bitten in our area, although one bloke died from snakebite near the airport in 1956.

My dad was quite choosy about the snakes he wanted. When I was around eight years old I used to hunt snakes close to my home and when I found one I'd get Pop to come and catch it, but he often put the skids under me because he didn't want them. Just four houses from us there was a narrow rock ledge where two brown snakes lived. Dad never wanted them and let them stay there and enjoy themselves.

On what is now Bilga Crescent on the ocean side of Long Bay Gaol, there were huge rock boulders where we regularly watched up to three browns sunning themselves close to ledges, but they would retreat quickly when they were disturbed. The rocks are long gone, to make way for more houses. I wanted Dad to catch one of those brown snakes, but he just grinned and said he didn't want any. I was young and thought you should catch every snake you saw. I didn't realise that most caught snakes were never taken home: the placid ones were released and the lively ones kept and used for the La Pa snake show.

Despite having been bitten several times himself, Pop kept 'fresh' snakes for the La Pa shows. The more you handle snakes, the more placid they become and the less exciting for the crowds at a snake show, so you wouldn't capture a snake for the show if it was already quiet. He also thought that if the snakes looked too quiet and calm it could give people, kids especially, a false impression of how dangerous they were—and that could get them into trouble if they found a snake and thought they could handle it.

These days there are rules restricting snake handlers from continually catching and releasing their stock to find lively ones. Back in the day, some of Dad's snakes would go to Taronga Park Zoo for display or be given or sold to travelling showmen, who would always hunt down Dad for fresh stock.

I think I was about eleven when I started catching snakes again (after the incident when I was much younger). At first I caught a monster black but he was too large, heavy and cranky and I couldn't handle him so I gave him his freedom. Around the same time I grabbed a 5-foot brown, which also scared me. I had some schoolmates with me, though, so I couldn't back off! I 'wanged' it, as we used to say—grabbed it by the tail and spun it around in a circle above my head, spinning around with it.

My mates ran to get a corn sack to put it in and by the time they came back the snake was giddier than me and I had no trouble bagging it. It was my first large brown and I was so proud, but unfortunately I couldn't tell Pop because I would have been in big trouble. So we told him it was caught by my big brother George, who then happily collected the reward money from Pop to go to the movies on his own.

Around this time, a newly migrated English family, the Hosmers, were living in a large tent and caravan about four doors down from us. There were two sons: Dennis, who was my age; and Bill, who was much older. We used to hunt together for snakes; Dennis and I would catch them while Bill held open the bag to drop them in. In later years Bill became an internationally recognised herpetologist, although as far as I know he never mentioned in his writings that he was inspired by watching Pop handling snakes in his backyard pit at La Pa, just 100 metres from where they lived.

The family eventually moved away up north, where Bill joined up with Louis Robichaux, a friend of mine. Louis showed Bill Hosmer a new undocumented skink, which he said he was going to send—along with a few more creatures—to Eric Worrell to 'describe', and asked Bill not to tell anyone until he'd done so. In the natural history world, describing a reptile (or any other living thing) is what it says it is: you describe it in minute detail, including size, shape and distinctive markings, and then you get the description published, preferably in a peer-reviewed journal. After that you may have established a new species or subspecies.

Bill had other ideas, though, and sent it to J.R. Kinghorn, who had recently retired from his position as assistant director and reptiles curator at the Australian Museum. Kinghorn described the skink and named it *Egernia hosmerii* in recognition of Bill. This was a sore point for many in the game because he'd broken his word to Louis, but we were just kids at the time and, to this day, the species is known as Hosmer's skink.

A great place to find snakes was east of the tramline along the high brick wall around Long Bay Gaol. The eastern side had a long billabong about 10 metres wide with large green reeds.

There were plenty of frogs around in those days, which attracted both brown and black snakes, and they had no predators. There was a metre-wide track between the reeds alongside the wall, where black snakes used to lie, although they would quickly slither away when approached. Sometimes, however, they would go for the wall, making it possible to catch them, which was made easier by the fact that the foundations were decaying and cracks and holes meant you could often grab one.

Years later the wall fell down is some places and eventually a new brick wall was built. There were always a few locals inside as inmates, usually for some minor offence, and they trained to become bricklayers by building the new wall. The gaol rewarded them with a packet of tobacco for any snake they caught or killed while they worked. So they got us to leave a small, 30-centimetre or so long snake in a bag or box at night, usually with a small wad of tobacco for their use, hidden either under one of their mortar boards or some bricks. They would find the bag the next day, gingerly remove the snake and claim a reward for its capture and killing.

Not far from the main buildings in Prince Henry Hospital, near the northern end of Little Bay Beach, was the Leper Home, a large low building with a high rusted iron fence. As the name implies, it housed sufferers of leprosy and was remote from the hospital because of the supposed risk of contracting the disease through contact with the sufferers. All the authorities knew then was that it was infectious and hard to cure. Now we know it's not that easily transmitted and can be cured with antibiotics.

We were young and fearless, though, and happy to mix with the patients. We played billiards with them and they gave us loaves of freshly baked bread. We had a lot of sympathy for these blokes and suggested to the old retired soldiers living on Bare Island at La Pa that they visit them and play billiards. This happened more than once, and everyone was happy. About 100 metres up the hill from the Leper Home, Dad showed me the remains of the hut his old friend 'Snakey George' had lived in, and told me how he'd become a second father to him (much to the irritation of his grandfather).

Along the ridge towards Little Bay, there were stacks of rusty iron that were very happy hunting grounds for Pop and me. Strangely there were no tiger snakes, just browns and blacks. The hospital staff had signs erected near the beach steps warning people of the brown snake danger. A few years ago, Randwick Council erected a similar sign near Malabar Beach, but I just happen to know that you're more likely to see a black snake there.

The Chinese market gardens at Botany were home to probably the biggest tiger snake colony in all of Sydney, although there were also a few swamp or marsh snakes there. A friend caught one enormous swamp snake that Dad displayed at the La Pa show. He made great play of its size and probably even pretended to have been bitten by it.

On the western side of the gardens was what we called Death Adder Hill. Ray Mascord, the author of numerous books on spiders, caught two death adders there. Adders weren't that common, and it was tigers that really predominated on the low lands. These days the locals will tell you they've never heard of Death Adder Hill. I suppose the name wouldn't have done much for real estate values and was just allowed to die. There aren't so many snakes around the area these days. Poor buggers, their food has gone—the waterholes have dried up so there are no frogs.

In later years, one of our main reasons for catching snakes was to give them to Eric Worrell's reptile farm, where he used to milk them for venom that the Commonwealth Serum Laboratory used to make antivenom. Eric had grown up to be a good friend of Pop's, and opened the Australian Reptile Park near Gosford in 1959. It has since been moved to the main north–south freeway, where you can't miss it—there's a huge model dinosaur on the western hill. We also kept a few snakes at home for Eric, and he used to come and milk them every fortnight. It's a bit stressful for the snake but they would live for a few years, and it was all about saving human lives.

Everybody has their own system for catching snakes. Half of it is knowing where to search in the first place. On the way there, you look 10–15 metres ahead, depending on the terrain. And then you look closer to the ground and, when you get to the spot, you look again. It depends on the situation, but my mate Jimmy McGregor and I once caught 163 tiger snakes in nine hours on Sylvester Smith's property at Lake George near Canberra. Jimmy was the spotter and I was catching and bagging them up. I remember saying, 'For Christ's sake, slow down, let me get them in the bag before you pin down another one.' I even caught a stack of tiger snakes on my honeymoon. Helen was less than pleased and retreated to our caravan.

A couple of funny reptile stories spring to mind. One weekend in 1949, when I was eleven, Pop took me by train to Bomaderry near Nowra and then we walked 15 kilometres to a favourite campsite near Greenwell Point. He recalled being there twenty years earlier with his mate Frank Rodgers. Frank owned the roundhouse shop at the La Pa snake pit. It was Frank who drove Pop to hospital on his truck that time he was bitten by the brown snake. Many years before, Frank's father had persuaded Professor Fox to set up the snake pit to drum up business for the shop (which has long since burnt down).

Twenty years earlier they had chopped away a knothole from a fallen tree so they could catch a giant red-bellied black snake. Sure enough, the tree and the axe marks were still there, and so was another 2-metre black, which Pop quickly bagged.

We spotted another giant black slipping into the reeds around the dam, so Pop rolled up his trouser legs and walked into the 15-centimetre-deep water in pursuit. Holding the 2-metre monster by the tail, Pop realised his legs were unprotected and yelled 'Pull down my pants!'

He meant for me to pull down the folded trouser legs, in case the snake curled back round and bit him. But before he knew what was going on I had his pants undone and floating around his ankles. It was a while before he could see the funny side.

Years later, when I was working on the powerlines, I used to catch snakes and sometimes goannas for Dad and Eric. I'd crate them up and bring them back on my occasional trips to the city. Times were different then and I was always picking up hitch-hikers; it never ever bothered me in the slightest. One day I stopped for a bloke who told me he was going to Central Station in Sydney to get on the midnight paper train to Goulburn.

'Hop in,' I said, glad of the company.

It was a hot night and we were driving along, when 'Paaarrrp!', he broke wind and it was a stinker.

'That was a beauty,' he said, blithely.

'Yeah, wasn't it?' I replied, as I rolled the window down, wondering if this joker had any manners at all.

Half an hour or an hour later, 'Paaarrrp!' again, and the vehicle smelled like something had crawled inside it and died.

'Oh, another beauty,' he said, shameless.

'Yeah, wasn't it,' I said, thinking to myself that if he did that again I'd kick him straight out of the car.

We were coming down onto the Harbour Bridge when 'Paaarrrp!', off he goes again. I'd been planning to run him all the way to the station, but after this I thought, 'He can find his own way!' As soon as I got through the toll gates I pulled over and said, 'I've got to go this way.'

'Okay, thanks mate,' he said, got out and off he went.

I only went around a couple of corners more, wondering what kind of bloke it was who stinks out his ride to the city, when 'Paaarrrp!' It was the goanna. I felt like chasing the bloke through the city to tell him it wasn't me.

CHAPTER 12

SNAKEBITES

THERE'S PROBABLY NO LINE OF BUSINESS IN WHICH THE PHRASE 'WHAT DOESN'T kill you makes you stronger' is truer than snake handling. If a snakey survived a slight bite and no antivenom was given, then pulled through okay with a few more bites and scratches, there's a slight possibility that they'll build up resistance to future bites. And they did get bitten. If you're in this game long enough, it doesn't matter how experienced or careful you are, sooner or later a snake will get you.

Pop was always turning his snakes over—getting fresh ones once the others had calmed down. The one exception to this rule was red-bellied blacks. Pop had a passion for these creatures and spent a lot of time on the south coast trying to find the biggest specimens he could. He captured a large one that ended up more than 2.4 metres long. It lived in captivity for eighteen years, but it could have been 40 years old for all we knew. Its

THE LAST SNAKE MAN

shed skin stretched to 2.75 metres and was sent to the Australian Museum, where for many years it was displayed in a glass case.

Pop was bitten throughout his career, including on the day he was photographed for the newspaper taking a tiger snake out of a tree. His technique was tried and tested: he grabbed each snake by the tail while the other hand flashed down to seize it behind the head, which he did successfully sixteen times. The seventeenth snake was sunning itself in a tree that Pop had to climb. Because Pop was restricted in his movement, the snake got him, but he just poured some antidote on the wound and continued as if nothing had happened. The pressmen were suitably impressed.

There had been times, however, when he'd suffered considerable pain and discomfort, such as when a large brown bit him on the nose at the 1924 Adelaide Show. When people asked if he was sick, Mum replied, 'Of course he was sick. He was always sick from snakebite.' He was once blind for three days after a tiger snake bit him on the knee. And many other times I watched in horror as the effects of venom became all too clear and he had trouble breathing normally and sat slumped in his chair drinking cold tea.

Once when we were snaking near Albury, Pop got bitten by a tiger snake but he didn't have a blade to scarify the wounds and bleed the venom. I remembered having seen a beer bottle a couple of miles back so I ran back and got it, broke it (after several failed attempts along the way) and he used the broken glass to cut a line between the puncture holes. I remember being embarrassed when we got on the train and he fell into a deep sleep and snored all the way back to Sydney.

Graeme Gow, who succeeded Pop as curator of reptiles at Taronga Park, recalls that in the late 1950s he borrowed a 1.3-metre tiger snake from Dad for a display and that the snake continuously struck at the wall of the glass tank where it was housed. When the time came for its return it took 90 minutes to get it safely bagged (partly because they didn't have a hooped bag).

When Graeme returned the snake to Pop, he warned him it was an angry one, earning him a look of 'Who do you think you're talking to?' before Pop tipped the snake from the bag. The tiger immediately flattened its head and struck at Pop's trouser leg. When he then moved it with his foot, the snake struck back, sinking its fangs into his Achilles tendon, and had to be forcibly removed.

Even so, Pop refused all offers of help and merely said to Graeme, 'Don't tell the missus.' His only 'treatment' was numerous cups of tea.

But a much more serious bite occurred in 1961, when a large brown snake bit Pop on the hand in front of a crowd at the Loop. He ignored it and carried on with the show, but 45 minutes later, while he was working with tiger snakes, Pop collapsed. The crowd thought it was all part of the act, but a friend, Frank Rodgers, realised there was something up and, with the help of onlookers, lifted Pop onto the back of his truck and quickly drove him to Prince Henry Hospital.

Frank told the doctors that the bite was probably from a tiger snake, as that's what Pop had been handling when he keeled over. For the first time in his life, Pop received antivenom, but there was no response. He was put on a respirator and his condition deteriorated rapidly. The antibodies that had kept him alive for almost 50 years were letting him down.

Luckily, a health inspector from Bathurst had seen the brown snake bite Pop but had left the show temporarily before Pop collapsed. When he came back and heard what had happened, he went to the hospital and told them the bite had been from a brown snake. When the correct antivenom was administered, Pop's body responded immediately and he was allowed to go home the next day. It's possible that Pop helped to some degree to save his own life, given the brown snake antivenom had only recently been developed and he had regularly provided Eric Worrell with brown snakes to produce venom for the Commonwealth Serum Laboratories.

Even after he retired from the zoo, Pop was still working with snakes and was constantly seeking an opportunity to return to the country around lakes George and Cowel, or the Murray River. Every September he and Eric Worrell would take a bushmen's holiday together to go snaking.

A few days after he suffered a stroke in August 1965, Pop rose from his bed in Prince Henry Hospital and disappeared.

He was found two hours later, walking through the nearby bush looking for snakes where, nearly 60 years earlier, he'd gone snaking with Snakey George. He passed away a couple of days later at the age of 68, one of the longest lived of his trade, at least before antivenom was developed.

For about a year before this, Mum had been asking me to take over the shows from Pop but I had never done snake shows before, and neither had my brother George. We just hunted snakes and caught them. But we realised once he had gone that if we didn't do it, an important old tradition would die with him, so, two weeks after Pop's death, George and I performed for the first and only time together at the La Pa Loop. After that, we worked the snake pit on an alternating roster basis on Sundays and most public holidays.

Although catching snakes can be a lot of fun, it has a serious side—and that's helping to provide venom for the labs so that they can create antivenom. That stuff isn't just for snakeys—there are plenty of people who live and work in the bush and find themselves on the wrong end of an angry snake. About two or three people each year die from snakebites in Australia, most of them from brown snakes, although Australia has the five deadliest land snakes in the world (based on how much of their venom it takes to kill a mouse). But there are a lot more people getting bitten than die—and that's because we

THE LAST SNAKE MAN

have antivenom and we know what to do when someone gets bitten.

Making antivenom is complicated but simple. A horse is injected with enough venom to give them a headache, probably. And then they slowly build up the doses, so that the horse develops enough antibodies to be fully immune. Their blood is then processed to isolate the antivenom. They rest the horse for a while and then repeat the process, but eventually they retire the horse to the paddocks.

It works with humans too. Theoretically they could have used Pop's blood to make antivenom, although that would have been for tiger snakes rather than browns or taipans. He'd been bitten so many times by tigers he'd become immune. A lot of snake men did. As I said earlier, a lot of them thought their antidote was saving their lives. They knew nothing about antibodies or that it was their previous bites saving them.

To prove this, a few years ago now, Charlie Tanner, a great snake man and a friend of the family, was injected with tiger snake venom by a chap from Melbourne University by the name of Dr Saul Wiener, who had already made the red-back spider antivenom. In the end Charlie was fully immune to tiger snake venom—enough to kill a dozen people would give him nothing more than a headache. And as long as they kept giving him little bites, that tolerance lasted forever.

By and large, the venom from different snakes carries different toxins, and some of the most venomous ones need their own specific antivenoms. Bites from other snakes with the same sort of venom, but nowhere near as toxic, can also be protective. There is a polyvalent antivenom for when they can't identify which snake the bite is from. It has saved people's lives, but it's not as effective as the specific antivenom.

I've read and heard it said on TV documentaries that snakes are immune to some forms of snake venom. This may be true for some, but it's also common knowledge that when some snakes bite themselves, a large swelling comes up on their bodies and can last for days. Years ago Mike Willesee made a documentary about me and Graeme Gow—I think it was called 'Deadly Australians'. Mike flew us out with his team to some red soil country out from Coffs Harbour. We took with us a large cranky mulga snake (king brown). It was a hot day and after a few takes the mulga went crazy, striking at anything and everything in range and accidentally bit himself savagely on the back. The snake soon became quite groggy and I soaked him in the Bellinger River for a while. We called the filming off and returned to Sydney. The mulga died the next day. There's no doubt in my mind it was the massive dose of its own venom that did it.

The inland taipan, or fierce snake, which is restricted to the corner country of Queensland, New South Wales and South Australia, is by far the most dangerous snake in terms of the potency of its venom. It's the most venomous snake in the world without dispute. And then comes the coastal taipan, the New

Guinea subspecies of which was named *Oxyuranus scutellatus canni*, after my dad.

A lot of experts have said that genetically this subspecies is virtually the same as the coastal taipan, but I think there's a lot more to the identification of different species than genetics. They can be morphologically, or physically, different, even down to the venom. This is an argument I'm having to this day over turtles. As advanced as genetics has become, I think there's still a lot to be understood. Many reptiles have been scientifically accepted as a different species when as far as we can tell their genetic make-up is identical.

Not only do different snakes species have different venom and different behaviours, but they're individually different too. Some snakes are characteristically quiet, while others are very aggressive, although I think 'defensive' is a more appropriate term. If it feels threatened, any snake can turn aggressive. Although, if roused, the brown snake and coastal taipan are more likely to attack, to some degree any snake is liable to strike if you really irritate it, like treading on it. The tiger snake is up there too, but the brown snake is the most defensive–aggressive of all our snakes and has a larger effective range, as it will strike with the full length of its body.

Snakeys cared more about the disposition of their snakes than the breed. Many snake handlers wouldn't work with animals that were too fresh and lively—it's difficult to talk to the public and manage an aggressive snake at the same time.

But pretty much all species quieten down tremendously after a while, and then you can handle them. In the old days, some snakeys had tiger and black snakes that had calmed so much they could put them around their necks or put their heads in their mouths, albeit with great care. Those tricks, which would never be done now, were performed by at least three of the early showmen I know of—and one of them was my pop . . . until a black snake bit him on the tongue. His mouth swelled badly and Mum had to feed him soup or water through a straw for days.

When I showed at La Perouse, I used to always use fresh snakes, just like Pop and my brother George did, because like them I didn't want people to see quiet snakes and think anyone could pick them up. I wanted them to see the danger. And I always had mad browns and mad tiger snakes so people could realise what they could really do.

I have a video of the last public show I ever did at the Loop in 2010. I took down my liveliest tiger snake, one that I only used to show now and then because he scared me. He was too good for me. As I picked him up, I explained to the crowd how dangerous he was.

'You know, people imagine they can hold the snake up and think they're better than the snake,' I said. 'Never. If the snake wants you, he's got you. And here's a typical example. I'll tell you what this snake's gonna do. He'll wriggle, like this, he'll come halfway up, and then he'll bite me on the wrist if he can.'

And that's exactly what happened. He wriggled, he came up, and he went straight for my wrist with his mouth open, but I rolled him over, and when he came down he was already in the bag. I wouldn't give him another go. I did my last ever show for the police down near Coogee Beach with my mate Andrew Melrose in 2016, and by then the mad tiger had settled down.

They train people in how to pick snakes up, but I never would. There are enough instruments and gadgets around that a person never needs to touch a snake to catch it. Some people say, 'You've got to learn to handle it, how it feels', but a number of learners and trainers have been bitten, and one nearly died, ironically by teaching people how to hold snakes.

CHAPTER 13

'HE GOT ME!'

I NEVER DEVELOPED RESISTANCE TO SNAKEBITE. IN FACT, I WENT THE OPPOSITE way: I became allergic to both the venom and the antivenom. The slightest trace of poison I received really knocked me rotten.

I've been bitten probably six times in my life, with a good number of close shaves. The first time, when I was in my early teens, I'd gone snaking with my dad, Ken Slater and Eric West down on the Murray River near Albury. Eric had a small reptile zoo at Tocumwal. Ken's introduction to snakes was via being a 'volunteer' at one of Pop's shows, where he had a carpet snake draped around his neck. It would be twenty years before they even exchanged names, but he'd got the 'reptile bug' and later become the first wildlife officer of Papua New Guinea. It was Ken who identified the New Guinea taipan and named it after Pop. Like me, Ken took every opportunity to go snaking with him.

We were out on this expedition when a tiger snake bit me on the hand as I was putting him in a bag. About five minutes later I walked up to the old man who was about 40 metres away and he took one look at me and said, 'You've been bitten, haven't you?'

When I said, 'Yeah,' he spun me around and kicked me up the tail. 'I told you, if it's too good, let him go.'

'How come he bit you?' Ken Slater asked, having a go at me, as they were driving me to Albury Hospital.

When the doctor went to give me the antivenom, he missed and it went all up the outside of my arm. Ken was a great snake man and scientist, and he had antivenom in an ice box to keep it cold, so the hospital used ours. But Ken went off his brain, telling the doctor what he was doing wrong and how antivenom was too valuable to waste.

Eventually the doctor said, 'Get out or I'll have you thrown out!'

'Okay,' Ken said. 'We're going outside. Just don't lose it this time or they'll report you, and if anything happens to John, it'll be on you.'

The next day I was out and I was all right.

Two days later Ken did a show at Eric's place on the way to Tocumwal, and was bitten by a tiger snake. Now it was his turn to go to Tocumwal Hospital for antivenom. We went to visit him and I sat on the bed.

'Ken, how come he bit you?' I asked.

'Piss off, you little smartarse,' he replied.

On the way back, we pulled up at a place called Tallangatta on the Murray River. It's under water now—they built another town when the Hume Dam was expanded and they raised the water level. Pop, Ken and I were in Ken's big Land Rover station wagon with all our camping gear jammed in the back right up to the back of the three seats in the front. Ken was driving and I was next to the passenger door, wearing shorts and a light T-shirt. Pop was in the middle, with his hat on as always.

We'd been through a paddock and got tangled up with some barbed wire, which had ripped the brake hose out so we had no brakes. We needed to get to a garage to get that all fixed but in the meantime we were trundling along, Ken using the gears to slow us down if need be. Suddenly he sings out: 'There's that brown snake, George.'

'What do you mean?' says Pop. 'What brown snake?'

'Behind me,' says Ken, looking in the rear-view mirror. Pop and I looked around to see a 5-foot brown snake, mouth open, right behind Ken's head. It was one we'd caught that must have escaped from its bag—and it wasn't happy. Quick as a flash, the old man whipped his hat off and flicked it sideways at the snake, which bit into the brim.

The next thing, Dad threw the snake at the windscreen. I was already scared, but when the snake hit the windscreen and dropped into my lap, I was petrified. Normally a brown snake would have gone mad and bitten the three of us several times until it got free—and this one was a big bugger—but I suppose he must have been stunned because he went into the little channel that the Land Rover has instead of a dashboard then he came along the windowsill. I was sitting stock-still with the snake right next to my face.

'Out the window. Get him out the window,' says Pop, but I wasn't moving. Then the brown snake stuck its head out the side window, which in a Land Rover slides from front to back. So I pushed more of his body through and *shoom!* I slid the window onto his tail. Ken dropped down through the gears and used the hand brake to stop the vehicle. And we got out and got the snake in the bag.

'And tie the bag friggin properly this time,' Pop said to Ken. But we laughed and laughed even though that thing could have bitten us a hundred times.

Every snakebite is different. The next time I got bitten it was by what they call a rough-scaled snake, also known as a Clarence River snake, because that's where they're most common. It's a very, very deadly snake. I was doing a free show for the Boy Scouts near Rylstone, just out from Mudgee, when the rough-scaled bit me on the finger. I put a tourniquet on, which was the done thing in those days (nowadays the advice is to apply a 15-centimetre-wide bandage to the full length of the affected limb under even pressure). The pain was terrible and after a while I took the tourniquet off. Straight away I got a lump up under my arm, from a swollen lymph node.

I thought I would be okay because I wasn't getting stomach cramps and I was only coughing up a little bit of blood. So we went back to where we were staying, at my mate Doug Kirkness's house. I went outside because I felt a bit crook, and a lot more blood came out of my mouth. I came back inside, feeling wonky, and said to Barry Nichol, another friend who was with us, 'Barry, I'm crook. I'm bringing up a bit of blood.'

Doug said we should go to the hospital but I said, 'No, we're going home to Sydney.' So Barry and I jumped in the car and headed homewards, but I felt really crook again and big lumps of blood came up out of my throat when I coughed.

'Pull up,' I said. 'You'd better take me to hospital.'

So we went back and saw Doug, and they took me to hospital. It was the worst bite I've ever had. I had stomach cramps and couldn't even talk, so they rang up Eric Worrell at the reptile park as he was our emergency number for snakebites.

'Give him a double dose of antivenom,' he said, and the doctors gave me tiger snake antivenom. It was a different snake but it was effective against the rough-scaled.

Although I couldn't talk, I could hear everything that was going on.

'He's going,' I heard Doug say. 'He's definitely going. His eyes are turned.'

I tried to say, 'Get f . . . ed!' They thought I was dying, and I thought I might be too, but, bugger me dead, the next day I was okay to travel and I came home.

That was when I developed the allergy. At first the hospital thought I had tetanus, but then they realised it was an allergy to the antivenom. I'd been given horse serum the time before, but it's usually the second time that an allergy develops. The antivenom had dealt with the snakebite okay, but it took stacks of adrenaline and antihistamines for me to overcome the allergy.

The next bite I had was at La Perouse, from a mad tiger snake. He was in the bag and I was doing it up. I always put the bag against my leg when I'm tying it and this one bit me through the bag and through my jeans. It was a very slight scratch and I said to myself, 'That was lucky—he never bit me.' But within about two minutes I felt giddy, and I realised I was so allergic to venom that the slightest amount was going to affect me.

'I'm sorry, folks, I feel a bit crook,' I told the crowd. 'I've got to go home.'

I packed up, went home and Helen drove me to the hospital, but I felt like I was in a light plane flying into clouds. By the time I got to Prince Henry Hospital I was totally blind. I'd always thought blindness was everything turning black, but for me it was white.

Helen got me in and then I collapsed on the floor. She told them I'd been bitten by a snake but at first the nurse and the sister refused to believe her. They pulled my dacks off, couldn't see any fang marks and decided I must have had a seizure. Finally a doctor who knew me came in.

'If this man said it was a snakebite, it was a snakebite,' he says. 'He's the snake man.' They gave me antivenom and put me in the intensive care unit, and the next day I was as fit as anything.

The doctor came in and said, 'How are you, John?'

'I'm perfect,' I said, as quick as that, which I was.

'We'll put you in another ward to see how you are for the day,' he said.

'Okay,' I said, 'but there are people in here dying everywhere and I feel good.'

While I was waiting to be moved, I decided to go for a walk even though I've still got the drip in my arm. As I came back, I could hear the nursing sister laughing her head off.

'You're not only the first bloke ever to walk out of intensive care,' she said, 'you're the first one I've ever seen walking out of the ICU with your drip on you.'

The last bite I had was from a black snake in December 1993. It's not a very deadly snake, although people have died in the past before antivenom was around. I came home and I was crook and it was really painful in my arm, so I rang up Struan Sutherland, the top researcher into snakebite venom back then. I told him it was only a black snake so it shouldn't have affected me so much.

'John, get up to Prince Henry Hospital,' he said. 'You're allergic to venomous snakes. Go to hospital.'

So I went to the hospital and saw Dr Hockin, the head bloke, and he decided not to give me antivenom, because of my bad reaction in the past.

'But you'd better stop overnight,' he said. 'We'll just watch your arm and see how you go.'

The hospital was in the process of being closed down at the time, so the number of available wards was restricted and they put me in the infectious diseases ward.

The next morning a different doctor came along and asked me how I felt.

'I'm real good,' I said.

'Oh well, you can go home if you want to.'

So I went home but I wasn't well at all, and my arm started going blue and then purple. I jumped back on the phone to Struan Sutherland.

'John, what have they let you out for?' he said. 'Get straight back to Dr Hockin. I'll ring him and tell him you're on your way back.'

Dr Hockin asked me why I said I was okay when I clearly wasn't.

'Doctor,' I said, 'you had me in the infectious ward. And all these blokes are coming in and sitting on the bed and saying, "Oh, tell us about your snake bite. What's it like?" You can't blame me for wanting to get out, can you?'

I was there for seven more days in the last of the general wards. The arm was getting really bad, and every day they were marking the spread of the purple colour with a pen. On Christmas Day, the doctor came in and told me they'd got a new antibiotic from Canberra but it was experimental and I had to sign a special authority if I wanted to get it.

'Pass me your pen,' I said. 'Where do I sign?'

An hour after they gave me the shot, the colour had gone down. Another hour and it had gone down even more.

'Do you want to go home for Christmas dinner, John?' the doctor asked.

'Bloody oath,' I said.

That was my last bite. Like I said, every bite affects you in different ways. Some might be really nasty and have you bringing up blood, with pains in the chest and cramps like you couldn't believe. Other times you might just go to sleep. They give you antivenom and you pull through—unless you're allergic, like me. The experts told me to get out of the snake game while I still could, but I kept going for another seventeen years, much to the frustration of my family.

I never got bitten again but I had some close calls. Once I was hit on the glasses, right on the bridge. I was doing a show and a brown snake went for my forehead and the next thing I knew I felt the hit on my face and my glasses were hanging off the cord I had round my neck. The snake was hanging off the glasses, his fangs still hooked over the frame. When I got the snake back in the bag I went up to my mate Robert McLean, who was in the crowd and asked him if there was any blood mark.

'No blood anywhere,' he said.

'Thank Christ,' I said. 'That was a scary one.'

Some snake handlers think they're too smart to be bitten, that they're too good for snakes. They don't know what they're talking about. They just haven't handled enough bad ones, that's all. A good tiger, brown snake or any of the taipans can be impossible to hold safely. If it wants to bite you, it will get you for sure. All the old pros will say the same thing as me.

When they want you, they've got you. And they all say the very same thing when they get bitten: 'He got me.'

George Cann, my pop, aged sixteen, already a fully fledged snakey.

My mum, Essie Bradley, also sixteen, as Cleopatra, Queen of the Snakes.

The La Perouse Loop in 1910. It was the roundhouse shop owner George Rodgers senior who persuaded Professor Fred Fox to set up the first snake show at La Pa at Christmas in 1897 to attract customers.

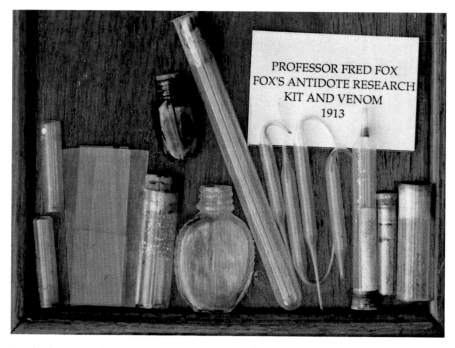

Snake bite antidotes were the stock in trade of the snakeys, but Professor Fox's couldn't save him from the deadly krait.

Snake handlers were enormously popular at travelling shows—this group had come all the way from America.

Essie and George at La Perouse—Mum was never all that keen on snakes, not that you could tell.

Macquarie Watchtower and Customs House at La Perouse, where I was born in 1938, photographed in the same year.

Me at two years old, with my pet python 'Fang'.

With my sister Noreen and our pet wallaby.

Our first house at Yarra Road, with Hill 60 and the power station in the background, in 1946.

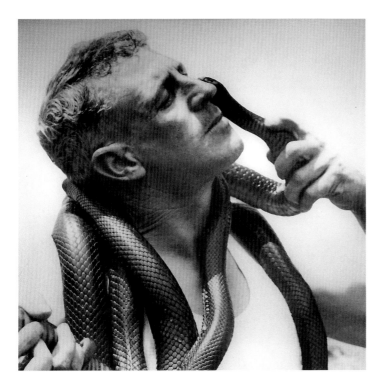

Pop in 1934 in the back-yard snake pit at Yarra Road.

My brother George holds me up, trapeze-style, in front of the snake pits.

Pop Cann at the La Pa snake pit, in the 1930s. Note the 'safety' fence and the 'Sunday best'.

Back from a trip to Lake Cowell, Pop adds some tiger snakes and a few browns to the snake pit. *(Pic: Eric Worrell)*

As a teenager, chasing a goanna on the dunes at the back of Congwong Beach near Botany Bay. *(Pic: Eric Worrell)*

Keeping a watchful eye as I handle a red-bellied black snake.
(Pic: Eric Worrell)

Pop Cann, with a New Guinea python, as Curator of Reptiles at Taronga Park Zoo. *(Pic: Eric Worrell)*

The NSW team (including Betty Cuthbert and a thirteen-year-old me) arrive in Hobart for the 1951 National Schools Athletic Championship.

In 1954, aged sixteen, winning the Australian junior 220 yards championship, in South Australia. My time qualified me for the men's heats and final. *(Pic: Keith Short Collection)*

Winning a 220-yard club race in Sydney just prior to the 1956 Olympics, beating two sprinters who were selected to compete in the games as well as the state champion. *(Pic: Keith Short Collection)*

Qualifying for the Olympic decathlon, I attempted the high hurdles and won. My friend, state champion Keith Short, was beaten for the first time in a year. *(Pic: Keith Short Collection)*

GANGWAY THE CANN WAY

'Gangway the Cann Way': a keen cartoonist, Keith Short poked fun at my technique . . . or lack of one.

This long jump of 7.44 metres was the best recorded for eight years. It convinced me to try to qualify for the Olympics in the individual event but I was injured in my first attempt.

MAIN STADIUM
MELBOURNE CRICKET GROUND

G 20
ROW SEAT
F 29

Nov. 28
1956
£1/1/-
INC. TAX

XVIth 1956

XVI OLYMPIAD, MELBOURNE
NOVEMBER 22—DECEMBER 8, 1956

A ticket to the Melbourne Olympics, which would cost $33 in today's money—a bargain!

Competing in the shotput in the decathlon at the 1956 Olympics.
(VPRS 10742/P0, unit 11, item B1286)

Winning my 100 metres sprint heat in the decathlon. My time was second-fastest overall. *(VPRS 10742/P0, unit 11, item B1216)*

Picked for the NSW Rugby League State Representative team v Queensland, 1960. John Raper, Norm Provan and Reg Gasnier were on the team and Clive Churchill was the coach! *(Pic: Sidney Riley)*

Third from right, front row, with the Tumbarumba rugby league team. *(Pic: 'Hippy' Quinn)*

Working as a rigger on the powerlines (and keeping fit) in 1963–64.

In full torso plaster
at Barry Goldspinks'
wedding in
Tumbarumba after
breaking my neck.
That was the end of
my rugby career.

Helen and me in 1959.

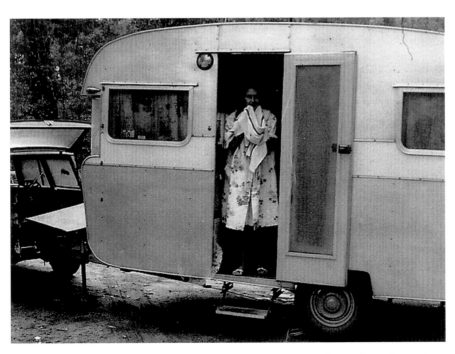

Helen in the caravan on our honeymoon, 1964. It was her refuge from the tiger snakes.

Pop with a fresh Chappell Island tiger snake. We ventured all over
the place on our snaking expeditions. *(Pic: Eric Worrell)*

My brother George (left) and me at the only snake show we ever did
together, after Pop died in 1965. *(Pic: Glen Blaxland)*

In New Guinea: Doug Kirkness and our Indonesian interpreter negotiating to buy a freshwater croc. The locals called them sweetwater crocs.

Bartering for animals in the Asmat region of Irian Barat. It became a spectator sport. *(Pic: Doug Kirkness)*

Our pig-nose turtle collection. They're each about 5 centimetres across. The red-belly turtles (*Elseya rhodini*) were not described until 2015.

With a tree kangaroo in the west New Guinea highlands, Irian Barat.
(Pic: Doug Kirkness)

Feeding a baby wallaby at Nabire, Irian Barat. Keeping the animals alive was one of our biggest jobs.

At the village of Otsjanep—note the canoe paddles that double as spears. The young warriors quickly painted their faces when strangers came by.

A typical shell nose piece—now on my study wall.

The village chief at Otsjanep wearing a dogs' teeth necklace.

Camped 100 kilometres up the Eilanden River, with two Indonesian soldiers and locals, hunting crocs for skins. *(Pic: Doug Kirkness)*

Searching the Mary River with John Greenhalgh. *(Pic: Helen Cann)*

Holding the first large Mary River turtle I caught. *(Pic: Helen Cann)*

The snake pit at La Pa in the 1980s. Note the too-close ice cream van.

Milking a snake for venom to send to the Commonwealth Serum Laboratories to make antivenom which would save lives . . . maybe even mine! *(Pic: Neville Burns)*

With an undescribed long-neck river turtle in the Kimberley Ranges.
(Pic: Steve Swanson)

On a camping and collecting trip to Gregory, north-west Queensland, with four mates in 2000.

Inspiring the next generation: my last show at the Loop, 18 April 2010.

(Pic: Steve Boys)

Federal MP (and Environment Minister) Peter Garrett and state MP
Michael Daley present me with a plaque to mark my final show.

(Pic: Randwick City Library Service)

CHAPTER 14

SHOWTIME

WHEN MY BROTHER GEORGE AND I TOOK TURNS TO RUN THE SNAKE SHOWS AT the La Pa Loop on Sundays after Pop passed away, we'd usually start around 1.30 p.m., but if neither of us could make it for some reason, I would put a sign up saying 'Sorry, no snakes today'. Sometimes we'd come down to do a show and there'd be 50 people waiting for us, so when I was away I'd get someone to put the sign up to make sure no one was hanging around waiting for a show that wasn't going to happen.

When we did the show we'd start by showing all the lizards— blue-tongues, shinglebacks, bearded dragons, Cunningham's skinks and always a water dragon—for the kids to pat and have a look at. The big water dragon used to just sit in the sun there with his head up in the air and stop there all day. He wouldn't move. I love him. He lives in the yard now and is more than 40 years old. He's a beautiful big animal, and they breed down there in my yard all the time. One of the babies that has grown up there, goes up onto the windowsill next door and scratches on the glass to alert Vanessa, my eldest son Paul's wife, wanting food brought out to it. They eat most kinds of meat, although sometimes they will find a mouse and have that.

After the lizard, we'd bring out a goanna and talk about the big goanna that bit me one time. I could never work out why he bit me, because he was a very, very quiet old goanna. The best reason I can come up with is that it was the day of the Bicentenary and there was a lot of stirring going on about politics and invasions and whatnot. The old goanna was a native of the country so he bit me. That was the only time he ever even tried to bite. Usually he'd lick your hands and do anything, but he got me that day and gave me 22 stitches. It hurt like hell, I can tell you, but I've had a lot worse than that.

Next we'd get the diamond or carpet snake out (or both) and walk them around and let the kids touch them. Then we'd move on to the venomous snakes. Sometimes, but not always, we'd take a death adder, but we would always do blacks, browns, tigers and copperheads. They were the four main venomous snakes. When the brown snakes came out we would take the hat around for coins.

The kids were always good. They always wanted to touch the lizards and even the pythons. Some of the parents would step back but the kids would want to touch them. That was really good, but I used to emphasise to them that not all snakes were like that.

'If you're not familiar with snakes, you can't tell whether it's a venomous snake or a non-venomous snake,' I'd tell them. 'There's no indication in any way to say he's got fangs or he's venomous.'

Then we'd talk about first-aid treatment. We started off by talking about tourniquets and how they found out the tourniquet was not effective but a pressure bandage worked, and so we'd talk about that. And we'd mention the research that was done in the bush by a couple of scientists from Darwin who found out that the ordinary 10-centimetre bandages were not as effective as a 15-centimetre bandage.

You must have a good bandage, and not one of the cheap crepe ones, and go along the limb a little bit tighter than was previously recommended. Every first-aid kit that was for sale at the time included a pretty lousy 10-centimetre bandage, and even snake men had brought in hundreds if not thousands of cheap narrow bandages from China and were still selling them. But at least they were better than nothing.

Each show used to take us about 40 minutes, except if there weren't many people because the weather was too hot or too cold, when we might take 30 minutes. No other snake men did a show that lasted as long as 40 minutes.

We never had any trouble with members of the public. Pop said snakes used to attract drunks at the sideshows, but the only trouble I ever had was from a really nice lady who was a bit of a drunk. She had the bladder from a wine cask in her hand and she was drinking and singing out and being annoying to the other people.

'If you don't go, I'm going to toss your grog away,' I said.

'Oh, you wouldn't do that, Johnny,' she said. But she kept on going and going, so I grabbed the flagon, spun around and threw it over the bank towards the beach. She went after it but she never came back.

The only other trouble I had there was with an ice-cream seller. They can be very, very annoying gentlemen. We used to like the ice-cream truck being there because people could get a drink and an ice cream while they enjoyed the show, but the drivers would pull their vehicle up right alongside the snake pit with their generators going to keep their fridges working. We used to say, 'Look, could you move away a bit? People will walk twenty metres for an ice cream,' but they didn't care. They wanted to be right on top of us and I didn't have a PA system so the crowd couldn't hear us over the engine noise.

One time this fella was in very close, probably about 2 metres from where I was working and I said to the crowd, 'He must be annoying you people,' and they all agreed with me about the noise, so I asked him to move. He just laughed at me, saying, 'You can't move me.' So I took a copperhead by the neck, stepped over the pit fence, grabbed the bloke by the shirt and said, 'Do you want me to fasten this on your lip?' and gave him a shove.

Well, he shot through but I'd say within ten minutes three or four ice-cream trucks pulled up, along with the police. He's got on his two-way radio and all the other ice-cream trucks in the district and the coppers had come to protect him. The police walked over alongside the wall and the crowd let them in.

'Can we have a yarn with you when you've finished your show?' a policeman said to me.

'Oh no. We'll have a yarn now, mate,' I said, 'so I can keep working.'

'This man said you grabbed him by the shirt and was going to put a snake on his lip,' the policeman said.

'A snake? You've got to be kidding,' I said and I bent down and I picked up a blue-tongue lizard. 'That's what I had in my hand and I never touched him,' I said. 'Ask the crowd here.'

'Yeah, he never touched him,' the people were shouting. 'He never even got out of the pit.'

Then the policeman said, 'Why don't you want him parked here. What's the problem?'

I was buggered for a split second but then I looked up and there was a sign there. 'There's a big sign on the pole here,' I said, pointing to the light pole on the corner. 'It says "No Parking".'

So the policeman went to the ice-cream seller and said, 'Hey, can you see that sign?'

'Yeah,' he said.

'Well, on your way before I book you,' says the copper, and away went the ice-cream bloke and all his mates.

That was the only trouble I had there at the La Pa loop in the 45 years I worked there. It was all pretty good—especially when you consider what all the old-school snakeys went through in their day.

CHAPTER 15

TURTLES

IF MY INTEREST IN SNAKES WAS INEVITABLE, THE BEGINNINGS OF MY PASSION for turtles was almost accidental. I first encountered turtles in Chinamans Creek near Botany Cemetery about 900 metres from my home in Yarra Bay. There are possibly no common long-neck turtles there anymore, but they may have returned now that contamination by the oil refinery run-off is no more. The first turtle I brought home was from east of Nowra, about 160 kilometres south of Sydney.

On the very snake-hunting trip where I pulled my father's trousers down, we walked the Pyree swamp and dams, near where we lived during the war—God, he could walk! I caught three long-neck turtles to take home, and I put them in a bag. There was often a bus to the Bomaderry train, and I would mind the bags with the tent, camping gear and snakes while Pop had a well-earned beer in a pub.

While I was waiting, an old Aboriginal man asked me what was moving in the bag. I let him look inside and he said he'd give me sixpence for each of the turtles. A done deal! I was horrified when Dad later told me the old man was going to cook and eat them. That was the last time I made that mistake. Later I collected a long-neck turtle at Chinamans Creek and put it in my father's frog pond.

Back then, these turtles were called tortoises. They're now known in Australia as turtles, because the term is more widely accepted round the world, and mainly because they live in water.

When I worked in the bush and the rivers were clear I would go snorkel-diving as often as I could. I have never dived in a more enjoyable waterway than upper Macleay River, where I used to swim when I was working on the powerlines in the area.

There were dozens of short-neck turtles in every waterhole, and sometimes platypuses and water dragons too, swimming near me. Water dragons—Australia's largest dragon lizard— would close their eyes under water, which was their way of hiding. It's a different story today in the majority of eastern water systems. Having survived and thrived for tens of thousands of years despite natural predators, human activities have led to a significant decline in the number of turtles and other river creatures.

The first interesting-looking turtle that I thought might be a new species or subspecies, I found on the Macleay River. It was similar to a Macquarie turtle (*Emydura macquarii*), the ones most commonly found in eastern Australian rivers and dams, but it was smaller. John Goode, the author of the 1967 book *Freshwater Tortoises of Australia and New Guinea* and considered by many to be the father of Australian turtle study, travelled with me to this river and was impressed with this small turtle. I sent one specimen to Hal Cogger, then curator of reptiles and amphibians at the Australian Museum, who wasn't sure what it was but agreed it was a form of Macquarie turtle.

Then I sent a photograph to Dr Archie Carr, the leading turtle and tortoise expert in the United States. He suggested I contact one of his students, Peter Pritchard, who asked me to send a pair of the turtles I'd found as well as a pair of Macquarie turtles for comparison. Fortunately, permits to send turtles overseas were easy to get, so I sent the specimens, despite the expensive postage. Later on he asked me to send more specimens but I was working on the powerlines and saving for a house at the time so I couldn't do it.

In the 1970s, Professor John Legler from the University of Utah was working in Australia on our turtles, and he travelled with me along the New South Wales coast looking at turtles. When we returned to his base camp at the University of New England, I asked him if he was going to describe all the coastal river Australian short-neck Macquarie turtles we'd seen as subspecies.

'You're joking?' he said. 'They're all different species.'

Sadly, Professor Legler never published that opinion and twenty years later I described them as subspecies, but some scientists to this day go to the other extreme and say they're all the one species, Macquaries.

* * *

Of all the turtles I've named or discovered, the one that may be my proudest achievement is a turtle that was utterly commonplace, yet took me on a quarter-century-long quest to reveal its origins. This was the so-called 'pet-shop turtle', hatchlings of which I'd first noticed in Sydney shops in the early 1960s. I later learnt that it had also been sold in shops in Brisbane, Melbourne and Adelaide for years before that. In some hobbyists' collections, they were beginning to acquire their own distinctive colours and form as they reached a carapace (shell) length of 100–130 millimetres. Meanwhile, hatchlings were to be seen every year scooting around Sydney's commercial aquariums.

Its natural habitat remained a mystery, however, and a puzzle I was determined to solve. When I first began my inquiries into their origins I was told they were imported from Torres Strait. This seemed possible but unlikely, and after seven or eight years I rejected that theory.

By the late 1960s I was sure the pet-shop variety was not closely related to saw-shell turtles (*Elseya latisternum*), as most experts and shopkeepers claimed. In 1974 I brought these turtles to the attention of John Legler, and for working purposes we gave it the name 'short-neck alpha'. It was only a matter of time, we reckoned, before its natural location was found and we would describe it in a scientific paper.

It would in fact be decades before the mystery of alpha's habitat was solved. Up until the time I spoke to Legler I had told only a few close friends of my search for the undescribed turtle. When my book on Australian turtles was published in 1976 I still made no mention of it. By this time, we were both convinced that alpha came from Queensland and we concentrated our efforts there (although Legler later considered it to be a possible native of Papua New Guinea).

In an effort to get more information, I tried to break the pet trade 'code of ethics' in New South Wales and Victoria. Pet shops rarely if ever revealed who supplied them with animals, partly because they didn't want anyone to set up in competition and partly because the legality of some animal trading was dubious. After I offered any two reptiles from my collection in return for information, I received a number of phone calls, but the leads turned out to be false.

John thought it better from a scientific point of view to seek help from museums and government wildlife departments. In 1980 the Victorian fisheries and wildlife department contacted me with inquiries of their own. New legislation regulating the trade in reptiles was being prepared, and the people framing it needed to know whether the pet-shop turtle was native to Victoria, from elsewhere in Australia or was introduced. I wished

I knew for certain, but I told them I was reasonably confident it came from Queensland. The following year I reluctantly broke my silence on alpha when I mentioned it briefly in an article on Australian turtles for *GEO: Australian Geographic* magazine.

The search was sure to hot up now that dedicated herpetologists came to realise they had an interesting undescribed turtle in their collections. It only made it more intriguing that this turtle had been living right under our noses for years. It was totally familiar and yet, from a scientific standpoint, unknown.

Not long after my article, I received a letter from Ric Fallu, the aquarium inspector for Victorian Fisheries and Wildlife in Melbourne. Still referring to the turtles as saw-shells, he told me that new state regulations had greatly reduced the number of hatchlings for sale, but that in earlier years, sales in Victoria had ranged from 3000–10,000 a year. Ric also gave me the name of a Melbourne aquarium owner he believed was the distributor for the state. I contacted the dealer, but he was as short with me as he had been with Fallu and told me nothing of any value before terminating our conversation.

Reluctantly, I pushed my hopes of discovering alpha's habitat to the back of my mind. It seemed my annual holidays of four or five weeks weren't long enough for a thorough search, although a number of three- and four-day trips allowed me to eliminate some possible locations nearer the ocean. A friend from Victoria went to Queensland, confident of making a discovery, while a number of Queensland contacts (some of them ex-traders) worked the pet shops looking for clues, all to no avail. Maybe Legler was correct and the turtles came from Papua New Guinea.

When one of my contacts gave me a likely location in Far North Queensland, I wasn't able to check it out. Legler did, but the 4000-kilometre round trip failed to locate any turtles. By the early 1980s my search was twenty frustrating years old. A breakthrough finally came, however, when wildlife enthusiast Gary Stevenson found a largish short-neck alpha in perfect shape and condition in Sydney's Centennial Park.

Approximately 200 millimetres long and obviously released sometime earlier, it appeared to be a subadult that had grown as nature intended rather than with human-supplied food. Having a turtle of this size to examine for the first time prompted me to phone the Melbourne aquarium proprietor once more, and this time he was relaxed and cordial, suggesting I try searching a lake near Swan Hill in northern Victoria. It was another false lead, but this time the round trip was only 2000 kilometres!

In 1984 the Victorian government passed legislation making it illegal to sell freshwater turtles with a carapace length of less than 100 millimetres, effectively stopping the import of hatchlings. This pleased me greatly, and I asked a friend to call in on the Melbourne dealer, who now had no reason to keep his information so close to his chest. Sadly, however, he had moved on and we couldn't locate him. By this stage the map I was using of Australia's drainage system had been almost obliterated by scribbled comments, crosses and question marks. Legler suggested I continue my search in North Queensland, but the area had been searched pretty thoroughly. As the list of possible habitats was reduced, however, I slowly became convinced that the short-neck alpha was from southern Queensland, west of the ranges. It seemed likely that alpha had not been found because it came from sandy-soil country where the rivers were perpetually clouded.

In 1987 I finally managed to track down the Victorian pet-shop owner. Since he was now out of the trade, he gave me the name of the Sydney contact from whom he received the turtles. Rather than phone, I wrote a long letter and sent him copies of my book and the *GEO: Australian Geographic* article. A fortnight later we spoke on the phone and he told me that the turtles were sent from southern Queensland as I suspected, they arrived around Christmas each year, and he would be back in touch after he'd spoken to his supplier.

I was over the moon, although two long months passed before I was given the name I'd been searching for—John Greenhalgh from Maryborough, Queensland. I wrote to John, also sending him a couple of my publications. Receiving no reply, I phoned him. He was quite polite and finally gave me a location for short-neck alphas in the bore drains around the town of Bollon in south-west Queensland.

The main waterway there is Wallam Creek. I had never heard of it, but maps showed me it's a 240-kilometre run of intermittent water that begins in Queensland and soaks about

100 kilometres into New South Wales in times of heavy flow, when it may even get as far as the Darling River. Of all the locations visited in my long search, this one excited me the most. It was in Queensland, in dirty water, and it was in the region where little research had been carried out. John Greenhalgh simply had to be telling the truth.

Since annual holidays are never long enough, I arranged some unpaid leave. Interest in the project was by now so great that Taronga Park Zoo in Sydney allowed its turtle expert, Chris Dorrian, to join me. John Legler was now back in the United States and, I allowed myself to think, would be informed of my triumph by fax. That was the plan but it was not to be the case.

After 2500 kilometres of hard driving I knew I'd have to be much more convincing before John Greenhalgh would pass on his long-treasured knowledge. On our way home, we visited the Condamine River, which John had mentioned in our conversation, but the water was clouded, it was approaching winter and water temperatures were probably too low for turtles. The Condamine would have to wait for another trip.

Meanwhile, I'd made arrangements to spend late September to early October of 1989 checking out as much of the Gulf and Cape York as five weeks would allow. With me was Graham Meredith, one of the few people who'd shown an interest in the short-neck alpha back in the early 1960s. The highlight of our trip was our meeting with John Greenhalgh, a big man of 76 years. I could instantly see he'd been around, and best of all I liked him immediately.

For weeks, I'd rehearsed this meeting in my mind. I couldn't afford to bomb it! When we introduced ourselves, and got over the formalities I asked John if I could do the talking, and at the nod of his head I had the floor for five minutes. When I'd finished he simply nodded once more and said, 'Okay, it's here in the Mary.'

John then told his story, and the more he spoke the more I realised he knew about this turtle, which he called a 'black head', referring to the dark cap on its crown. Since it was morning we decided to go straight to the river and have a dive, while John said he would show us some eggs. That said, John had already mentioned the eggs' incubation period was eight weeks, but I also knew the turtles hatched near Christmas and it was now only 30 September. As well as that, I still had my reservations about the Mary River. I'd dived there earlier, as had Gary Stevenson, John Legler, Patrick Couper of the Queensland Museum and Steve Swanson, who used to buy pet-shop turtles even though he actually lived on the Mary.

Nevertheless, my adrenaline was pumping as Graham and I arranged our diving gear. The water was extremely cloudy, as the river was being sand-dredged for industry further upstream. John had already gone down to the eroded riverbank in search of a nest but was back within fifteen minutes, telling me we were a month too early. He advised us to come back on our return from the Cape.

We dived the river for about an hour, but in vain. Visibility was down to about 60 centimetres and we found only the northern snapping turtle (*Elseya dentata*) and Krefft's turtle (*Emydura krefftii*). After we'd driven John the 30 kilometres home, we returned to the river and checked another location, still with no results. After three hours of fruitless search I became convinced that John was playing games with us. He wouldn't have been the first naturalist to give a perceived rival a bum steer to protect a resource that only he knew about. We headed north.

On our way back, on 30 October, we were diving the Mary River again, but we didn't call in on John or check the nesting sites he'd shown us. Instead, we spent a couple of hours diving in adverse conditions, set a number of traps with various types of bait and settled down by a good camp fire.

As we reflected on the distance we'd travelled on this trip and the number of possible locations we'd eliminated from our search, I felt that no one else but us deserved to locate alpha. But, boy, they were trying! While we were up north, Chris Dorrian and a companion were checking out my next location on the Condamine River, just over the ranges!

During the following months, I kept in touch with John Greenhalgh and a bond seemed to develop between us. We certainly had some interests in common. 'Next season you'll get him,' he told me on the phone. Since John had told me of up to 15,000 hatchlings being incubated each year, with about sixteen to the nest, I agreed there had to be enough adults in the river for me to find one.

In August 1990, Helen and I left Sydney on a twelve-week round-Australia trip to photograph turtles and their locations. I'd planned to reach the Mary River in late October and keep in touch with John while we were on the road. There was a note waiting for me when we arrived in Humpty Doo at Gow's Reptile Zoo.

'I've got one,' John had written. Accompanying the letter was a photograph of what I thought to be an adult male alpha. One of John's many friends had caught it for me. We cut a week off our itinerary and headed straight for Maryborough. By the time we arrived I was as excited as it's possible to feel while still harbouring some apprehension. A search that had lasted for more than a quarter of a century was coming to an end. John greeted us, took me to a large drum in which he kept the turtle and removed the lid.

My heart sank. Inside there was just a medium-sized northern snapping turtle. My mind flashed back to the photograph I'd seen in Darwin and I thought of all the kilometres I'd clocked up over so many years—including more than 22,000 on this trip alone. I was speechless with disappointment and it must have showed. John held a straight face for about ten seconds then, with a grin, said, 'Well, if that's not him, look in this drum.'

It's hard to convey my feelings when I first looked at an adult pet-shop turtle. At last I was able to pick up one of the creatures I'd been searching for since the early 1960s. But although I never mentioned it to John, I still wondered if the old fox had had it sent from another river. I had to check.

By late afternoon we were on the river again, at another location, walking along the road, when John found a nest that contained sixteen smallish eggs. The first tracks of the female, probably made the previous night, and the depth at which the eggs were deposited indicated that she was large. The only turtle I knew of that size on the Mary River was the northern snapping turtle, but these eggs were obviously from a different species. In fact, I'd never seen eggs like them before. We buried them again, but I planned to return to them if I had no more success on the river. No diving was attempted that day as the water was cloudier than on my previous visits and I had ear trouble from weeks of constant diving.

Next morning, we were back on the Mary. John rowed while I dived, my depth restricted to 1.5 metres, where visibility was only about 80 centimetres. Still, I caught a number of other *Elseya* and *Emydura* species, much to John's surprise. My worries that the pet-shop turtle came from elsewhere still nagged me and, sitting in the boat, my ear aching, I was tempted to ask John to come clean. But I could see that he too was becoming frustrated. He said that he had reservations about catching one in these murky waters but was sure I would meet with success if I stayed for another couple of weeks!

After a late lunch, I walked a few hundred metres downstream with a pair of binoculars. I could see two large turtles basking on a log, but I was too far away to distinguish them. I crawled forward another 30 metres to a better vantage point and, sure enough, made a positive identification. The pet-shop turtle— John Greenhalgh's 'black head'—*was* native to the Mary River. Helen videoed the sighting and my reaction. The search was over.

The turtle really should have been 'discovered' years earlier, since it's found so close to Brisbane. The main north–south highway crosses the Mary River drainage system at a number of locations and is never far from the river itself.

Not only that, but the much-studied Queensland lungfish (*Neoceratodus forsteri*) is found only in the Mary River and the Burnett River immediately to the north. First described by Gerald Krefft in 1870, the lungfish can only be effectively caught with set nets, so it's likely that many pet-shop turtles were also netted. If so, they must have been released undescribed, since none had been registered at museums.

It had taken 25 years for a little curiosity to evolve into a search, then a quest and, ultimately, a race to discover the origins of arguably the best-known turtle in the country. It must have been my competitive instincts coming through, but I was glad it was me who both started the race and finished it.

CHAPTER 16

COLLECTING IN IRIAN BARAT

IN 1972, WHEN VIC DALTON AND I WERE INSTALLING CAR-WASH EQUIPMENT IN petrol stations between work on the powerlines, we were travelling up and down the eastern seaboard from Queensland to Tasmania. We were in Hobart on 25 June in what would turn out to be the coldest day ever recorded there (close to –3 degrees Celsius in Hobart and –13 degrees Celsius elsewhere on the island). We were working at a wind-blown place and one of the garage attendants came over.

'One of you blokes John Cann?' he asked. 'You're wanted on the phone.'

'Who could ever be ringing me out here?' I thought. Helen and Vic's wife were staying in a boarding house we'd rented at Battery Point in Hobart, and I didn't think it would be either of them.

'It's the USA calling,' said the garage hand.

I was really concerned, so I quickly jumped on the phone. It turned out to be my mate Doug Kirkness. I used to work with Doug's brother on the powerlines and he'd introduced us because of our common interest in snakes and wildlife generally. Doug had done an apprenticeship as an electrician, and when he got his papers he'd asked me to help him find a job. I had a look around but all I could see was work in Papua New Guinea, so he ended up finding work in Port Moresby. Doug would go on to build his own electrical business and have a chain of health studios, but that was all to come. Why was he calling me? And what was he doing in the United States?

'I'm ringing from Houston, Texas,' he said. 'A chap who used to get some reptiles and animals off me in Port Moresby has flown me to America in payment. Now he wants me to go to Irian Barat to collect more specimens. Do you want to come with me?' Irian Barat is now known as Irian Jaya or Papua, and is the other side of New Guinea island from Papua New Guinea, and under Indonesian control. (Although I have to admit that at the time I thought it was somewhere in the Middle East!)

'Yeah,' I said, looking outside where it was freezing, but then I thought about it. 'No,' I added. 'I've got a contract up in Goondiwindi.'

'Well, I won't take no for an answer,' he said. 'When are you going back to Sydney?'

'Four days.'

'Okay, I'll ring you at seven o'clock when you get home.'

'Ring me, but I can't go. We've got this contract on.'

Doug said he'd ring anyway, because it was the chance of a lifetime and he was sure I'd change my mind. When I told Vic about the call he said I should go, but he had no one else to work with him and he didn't want to lose the contract. I'd resigned myself to telling Doug I couldn't make it when the very next day, Vic's son, a competent fitter who'd been in detention at Puckapunyal army base as a conscientious objector against the Vietnam War, was released.

'Well, my son can take over,' Vic said when he heard the news. 'Do you want to go to Irian Barat?'

'Oh yeah,' I said. All I had to do was explain it to Helen. Bindi, our youngest, was only a few months old so Helen, unsurprisingly, wasn't too keen. But she realised this was, as Doug said, the chance of a lifetime—and the money on offer was good too.

Doug, the bastard, didn't ring until nine o'clock. I was anxious by then because I'd made up my mind. He told me he was just teasing me, because he knew I really wanted to go. He asked me how much I was earning. At the time I was making about 50 bucks a week, tops.

'What do you reckon if we give you 150?' he said.

I couldn't believe it. I said, 'You've got me.'

'I knew you'd change your mind,' he said. I didn't tell him he hadn't needed to try.

We were supposed to be going for six weeks. As it turned out, I got back six months later. The idea was that we'd be bartering dollars, salt, trinkets, coffee, tobacco and sugar with some fairly isolated tribespeople, to get their help in catching rare animals for a dealer by the name of Leon Leopard (yes, really!) who supplied animals to United States zoos. Apart from the adventure, the financial rewards would be pretty good. It was a win-win.

Okay, there was a risk involved. This was only a few years after Michael Rockefeller, an adventurer and anthropologist— and the son of American multimillionaire Nelson Rockefeller, Governor of New York State and US presidential candidate—had gone missing on an expedition in the area.

Before we went, Leon Leopard gave us photos of the animals he wanted for the United States zoos, and for which they had permits. The idea was that we'd show the locals the pictures and they'd go and get the animals for a reward.

We travelled all over the country by plane, canoe, steamship and foot. I still have nightmares about swimming in crocodile-infested waters too muddy to see more than a few feet in front of me. But it was, indeed, the trip of a lifetime, maybe several lifetimes, with a bit more adventure and a bit less reward than we'd planned for.

★   ★   ★

The trip didn't get off to the best of starts. I'd put both of our air tickets on top of the fridge but when I went to look for them the night before our departure, they were gone. I thought my brother George had taken them as a prank and I went mad at him, but he denied all knowledge. We hunted high and low, tore the house apart looking for those tickets, but couldn't find them anywhere, and the next day we had to beg the travel agent to issue new ones. Years later I moved the fridge to discover they'd dropped down behind it.

Losing the tickets wasn't the worst of it. When we left, we had to take a stack of cash with us for all our expenses. This was long before internet banking and the like, and we probably broke the law by taking so much money out of the country, but it didn't matter so much in those days. Doug came over here from the United States with US$25,000 in his bag to pay for the expedition, and the police arrested him in Los Angeles because there'd been a lot of money stolen in a big robbery there. He missed his flight, of course, and he had to convince them that it was all legitimate. But a couple of phone calls to the bank where the money was withdrawn, and bingo, he was on the next plane out of there.

The next issue was taking so much money into Jakarta, where you were only allowed to bring in a small amount of foreign currency. But there was no such thing as body searches, so I had money in my shoes and socks and in my pockets. All this money was to buy animals, to hire planes to transport them, for our own airfares on little planes, and hotel expenses when we were in towns.

As we spoke no Indonesian, we had great trouble convincing government officials used to highly organised scientific expeditions that we were not only serious but genuine. Tourists weren't allowed into Irian Barat and anyone given an entry permit was thoroughly screened. We had to undergo more interrogations than you'd believe possible. By the time the run-around was over, two weeks of our original six were gone.

* * *

When I got there, I'd posted back home a magazine from the plane, with a feature about cannibals in it. It was weeks before it arrived, and I didn't realise we'd be gone for months with weeks between communications, so at one point everyone was convinced that we'd been killed or taken. One of my kids saw the magazine, looked at the picture on the front and said: 'Is that the man who ate Daddy?'

In fact, there was cannibalism but it was neither random nor widespread. By that time, river travel was reasonably safe, as the missions and the Indonesian Government had banned headhunting and cannibalism. When cannibalism was practised at all, as it still was in some remote areas, it was usually part of an elaborate religious revenge ceremony conducted when an enemy who'd done some harm to the tribe was executed then at least partially eaten. And that's what I believe happened to Michael Rockefeller.

A lot of books and magazine articles have been written about this, but I met an indigenous chief who was there and part of the whole thing. In fact, he gave me the bone that he, the chief, had through his nose, and it's hanging on my study wall right now. The story goes that Rockefeller had been in the country collecting specimens and photographs and shooting films. He was doing a lot of filming in the highlands but the one thing he didn't have was film of a battle between two tribes. They're very warlike people but it just happened that at that time there was no feud going on so there was no battle to film.

So, according to the missionaries who talked to me, Rockefeller paid two tribes to have a battle with spears, bows and arrows and clubs so he could film it. At this point the story gets a bit confused. Some said there were a lot more injuries than they'd anticipated, others say that Rockefeller said he'd only agreed to pay so much for so many men but a lot more turned up and he refused to pay the extra ones.

According to the bloke who told me, Rockefeller headed off with his film and artefacts and left the tribes to deal with it. Now, in Asmat, on the island's south-western coast bordering the Arafura Sea, the tribesmen were already angry because some time before, Dutch soldiers had come through and shot up a village and killed a few locals. Rockefeller had nothing to do with that but his catamaran, built from native canoes, capsized a few clicks offshore from the village. He used some jerry cans as floats and swam for the shore, telling his mate that he'd get help.

A book that came out a couple of years ago claimed that as soon as he got ashore, the locals put a spear through his gut and an axe through the back of his head, killing him, then performed a ritual on his body and ate bits of him. According to the chief I'd befriended, however, he was captured and tied up, and they cut off, cooked and ate bits of him while he was still alive.

I also made good friends with the man who was in charge of that area, Simon, a very well-spoken Indonesian who knew all about it. He said it was payback for villagers who were shot by a Dutchman, and Rockefeller was the first white man who'd turned up since. They kept him alive, tied him down, cut meat off him, and cooked it and ate it. One missionary I spoke to, Dr Ken Dresser, in reference to the staged battle, said: 'He got what he deserved.'

The Rockefeller family has always said that Michael's body was never found because he drowned at sea and never made it to the shore. They had a helicopter search done for his body, and his father flew into Biak, an island just off the northern coast, in his own Boeing 707, then made his way down to the Asmat area. There were stories flying around about what really happened, but the Indonesians always denied them. Rockefeller met local officials in Asmat, had private briefings with them, and 24 hours later went home. That convinced me that he was pretty sure of what had happened to his son. Would he fly all the way over there to look for him and go back only 24 hours later?

Quite a few years after I was there, there was a call for information in the Sydney *Sun* newspaper. An investigator was being paid by the Rockefeller family, and if anyone knew anything about what had happened to Michael, they were requested to ring the investigator at his hotel. So I rang him up.

'Yeah, I know a fair bit about him,' I said. 'I've got photographs and I know exactly what happened. If you want to come out and see me, I'll give you my address.'

'Okay then, I'll get in touch with you,' he said. I gave him my phone number but I never heard from him again. I reckon he was just going through the motions, maybe for publicity or so he could charge his client, and never expected anyone to ring him up. He must have got a shock when I told him I knew the whole story.

*　　*　　*

Initially we flew to Biak Island, north-east of Irian Barat, where we spent two days organising wildlife for our later return. From there we flew direct to Jayapura, the capital, where we needed to locate various animals. We spent a week there with little success, but we started to put our collecting process together. We realised the best way to obtain information was to make contact with missionaries and their pilots, and we worked out that we'd have to go further south for crocodiles and brolgas, and to the highlands for tree kangaroos and giant echidnas. For the rest of the required animals, we'd have to rely on chance, and where transport could take us.

We then flew to Merauke on the south coast, close to the border with Papua New Guinea. Back in 1972, the only way to travel along the coast was by ship. Traders travelling from Merauke to Agats, where we wanted to go, are available only every two months, but we were lucky. The next night a ship berthed that was due to travel that route. I'll never forget the next three days. I had five stitches in my hand and they'd broken open, while Doug's complexion was continuously green from the rough sea swell and the stink of the ship.

The ship was basically a freighter, and it had one toilet and one shower for 150 passengers; the rest of them were all crammed under a tarpaulin on the deck, but we were lucky to get a cabin below, even if we had to sleep on the floor. The whole place stank like a sewer and I held off going to the toilet until late at night and then hung over the side of the ship, with my backside exposed to the sea, doing what needed to be done. At one point I tried to have a shower. I got all my clothes off in the dark and went in holding my breath, standing up to my ankles in rubbish, but there was no water.

The trader was also a travelling menagerie. Cages containing a variety of animals including snakes and crocodiles littered the decks. At Agats, a village of stilt housing, a bunch of villagers clambered aboard, carrying bunches of live crabs and tortoises to be sold for food. We settled for crab. We went ashore and enjoyed a welcome wash and our first night's sleep since we'd got on board.

Next morning we rejoined the ship and steamed up the Eilanden River to begin our hunt for animals and set up base camp at a place called Josaker about 160 kilometres inland. To me, the highlight of the journey was a brief glimpse of the pig-like snout of one of our most keenly sought animals—the rare freshwater turtle, *Carettochelys*. This turtle was originally found only along the south coast of Papua New Guinea, living in the larger freshwater courses, but the largest numbers are to be found along the south coast of Irian Barat, and it's also now known from rivers in northern Australia. (It's worth noting that many of the place names have changed in the intervening years and some of the villages seem to have disappeared completely.)

Josaker made a good base because it had a mission with a transceiver and an airstrip. We settled in there, renting an okay hut, and the locals looked after us, but it was still hard getting food. There was plenty of fish but after a while we craved something else.

There were worse dangers than a boring diet, though. Doug, a local guide, an interpreter and I were on a trip up the Eilanden River in our 11-metre motorised dugout canoe, when the outboard motor broke down around 140 kilometres from the nearest safe village of Fos and couldn't be fixed. With three paddles and practically no assistance from a slow-flowing current, we set off in searing heat for a marathon trip downstream. Doug got badly sunburnt and, with his fair complexion, blistered up, so we were all pretty relieved as night-time approached to give relief from the direct sun and stifling heat.

We continued paddling in the dark and noticed a camp fire glowing around 100 metres away across on the other side of the riverbank—the river was as wide as 400 metres in places. Our guide asked me to flash our torch to signal to the camp, which I did. The response was immediate: a bullet whizzed past my head and into the riverbank beside us! Everyone hit the deck and we drifted until we reached a bend in the river.

That incident put us on high alert until we reached Fos at sunrise, our guides paddling nonstop. Luckily it was Sunday and the Reverend Bob Fraser arrived at 8 a.m. to hold a service. He invited us to join him on his large motorboat to go south to Josaker with him. For reasons we couldn't work out, however, he didn't ask our indigenous guide or interpreter to join us. He could have carried all of us on board and towed our canoe back to Josaker. Instead, Doug had to hire six locals to paddle their boat and ours down to Josaker from Fos, an eight-hour return journey.

Many of our boat journeys were sheer delight, with bunches of flowering orchids above our heads in so many different colours that they appeared like a fiesta archway. One time we went by canoe with an outboard motor to Sanggo, where the missionaries looked after us. We took a missionary's old chug-a-lug boat—it was a bit like the *African Queen* in the old Humphrey Bogart movie. We went past one village where the river was 200 metres wide and we were well out from the shore.

'Hide anything valuable underneath the decking,' the missionary said. 'The natives come across in their canoes and they take anything they want and we can't resist them. So if they come, give them what they want or they'll kill you. Make sure anything of value is hidden. But if they want your shirt, you've lost it.'

They never came. There seemed to be no one in that village at all, and it was a big village too. We had no trouble there whatsoever.

On another trip, up the Eilanden River, we towed a canoe carrying four hunters for 32 kilometres. The canoes were lashed side by side and, much to our discomfort, a host of dog-meat crocodile baits were tied to the sides of our passengers' vessel. The leader of the group, Watamena, an elderly man from Biak, spoke only Indonesian with our guide. As we rode along, Doug and I spoke to one another about the local hunting methods and how we thought they were barbaric. When we camped at nightfall, Watamena suddenly turned to me, asking in perfect English, 'How many crocs do you want, Mr John?'

Doug and I were dumbstruck and embarrassed. Watamena made no mention of our criticisms, but said that during the war he'd spent five months with the Dutch Navy in Sydney. While he was there, he said, he'd twice spoken to the Snake

Man of La Perouse. I still find it hard to express my amazement that there in the middle of the New Guinea jungle was a man who 30 years before had spoken with my father at home. We learnt that Watamena was a linguist, speaking four languages perfectly, and he was a wonderful help. He ensured we had as many crocodiles as we needed, and even helped us to obtain the *Carettochylys* freshwater turtle.

The reason the six weeks turned into six months was that it was very hard getting all the animals we wanted. We didn't do that much trapping ourselves, although I did catch some of the freshwater crocodiles when the tides dropped and I could sneak up on them when they were basking on thick tree branches that they would swim onto when the tides were high and be left there when the tide was out. Doug would distract them in the canoe while I swam downstream towards them.

We recruited our collectors in each of the many different villages we visited. The people had seen very few Europeans, and young hunters armed with bows and arrows would return each evening with introduced deer or other game across their shoulders. When we showed them the photos, they'd turn them over and look behind them to see where the animal was. They'd never seen photographs before. There were lots of photos—of birds of paradise, tree kangaroos, pig-nose turtles, blue-winged kookaburras, lizards and so on.

One of our interpreters, Martin, was Indonesian and lived in the jungle on the south coast. When we were further up the river, we picked up another interpreter for some of the tribal languages. So there were four of us: them, Doug and me. We traded fish hooks, salt and tobacco—we had a kerosene tin full of tobacco someone gave us—and the locals would come in with lizards, snakes and other animals. Sometimes the snakes they brought in were too damaged and we'd say 'No, it's dead' or 'Devil' or 'Damaged'.

We never had more than a few small turtles, so we didn't need tanks. We did have one big pig-nose turtle that I kept in a toilet bowl for a couple of days when we were staying with the missionaries. There was nowhere else, so I flushed the toilet nice and clean and put him in the water. The smaller ones I could just put in a bowl and they could travel for days just on slimy damp material until they got back to America.

On one expedition up the river, when we landed the locals put on a display for us of how they used their oars, which were sharp at one end and doubled as spears, for either hunting or tribal warfare. They threw them by taking a longish run and hurling them javelin-fashion at a target.

After they'd finished, I asked if I could have a throw. It was fifteen years since I'd thrown a javelin in anger, but I was pretty fit and you never lose the technique. I took about five steps and flew the spear way past the marks reached by the very best of the local throwers. They were amazed and asked me to show them again, probably because they thought it was a fluke. I did and they seemed pretty impressed as the spear disappeared into trees at the end of the clearing. If this had been a Hollywood movie, I would have been declared a god. As it was, I was happy to receive their praise and a free meal of fish and sago.

Another hairy moment was when we travelled down to where the Eilanden and another river meet, down from the Rockefeller village. When the tides are strong, the counter-flows create a massive whirlpool at the confluence, and we had to use the motor outboard in full reverse to overcome it. Even so, we were swept around two or three times and we thought we were goners. On the way back, we gave the whirlpool a very wide berth.

For all these physical dangers and the occasional culture clashes and communication problems, they weren't the biggest obstacle to our success. Good old Third World bureaucracy and corruption were about to rear their ugly heads.

CHAPTER 17

A CRUEL END

ONE OF OUR PROBLEMS WAS HOUSING AND FEEDING THE ANIMALS WE'D COLLECTED. We had many specimens from the Asmat district, but finding enough food to keep them became a problem. We decided to leave Josaker and try to fly to Merauke. The next day a powered canoe arrived from Agats and we were given a bill for $50 to be paid to the local authorities. As we needed our local currency, we gave the bearer $60 in US currency. This generosity was our undoing.

The next day, five uniformed soldiers arrived and presented us with a bill for a further $200. After a discussion with Doug, I went into the other room, folded a couple of sheets of paper and placed them in an envelope on which I wrote on, 'Not this time, mate'. While drinking a cup of coffee under the watchful eye of the 'debt collectors', we folded $200 into another envelope, then Doug distracted them by displaying some snakes while I switched envelopes. They left and we had an uneasy night.

Fortunately, tides prevented the 'debt collectors' returning as soon as they might, and at 11 a.m. a plane, chartered for us by the mission, arrived to take us to Jayapura, as smoke made all flights to Merauke impossible. We learnt later that both demands for money were illegal, but given the circumstances, we still wonder what might have happened had the aircraft not arrived. Sadly, that wasn't the end of the corruption we encountered.

Our specimens fell into two groups: the protected and the lucky. Why lucky? Because the non-protected species got out of Indonesia alive, thanks to being looked after by a bloke recommended to us until they were ready to be shipped out. The protected species, however—the rare animals—had to be approved by the Indonesian Institute of Sciences (LIPI) and kept at Jakarta Zoo until they were ready to be sent to American zoos under the permits we carried from them.

Doug had met a Mr Galston, the director of Jakarta Zoo, several times and explained what we were doing. Galston was very encouraging and supportive from the get-go. Unfortunately, he turned out to be more of a snake than any of the reptiles we'd collected.

We took the first load of protected animals through to Jakarta and, while I was interviewed by the authorities there, Doug went back to Port Moresby where he had his business to look after. Despite all the arrangements having been made in advance, at LIPI I was interrogated on a daily basis about what we were doing, why we were doing it and who we were doing it for—every day it was a different bloke with the same questions, over and over. It took me six days and it was very hard.

Towards the end of the week I had to go south to Bogor (their scientific capital), so I took all my paperwork with me in a briefcase. The meeting was held in a monstrous long room with about six or seven government officials there, all dressed up in their suits and ties.

'John, we would like to ask you a few questions about West New Guinea,' one of them said.

'Sure,' I said. 'What's the trouble?'

'Do you have any maps there?' he asked. 'What are the airfields like?'

I pulled out this big map that I had and said, 'Well, all those red dots are airfields.'

This chap who claimed to be in charge of airfields or something came around the table and looked and said, 'That's bullshit. There's not that many airfields in West New Guinea.' He said I was looking at the red dots of the Church of England churches.

I told them that the Catholics had more airfields, but they refused to believe me. They seemed to know nothing about that country. They went away to get copies and came back ten minutes later. I asked him what he was so curious about. One thing they wanted to know was what the dangers were with snakes and so on. I ended up giving them information about where to get antivenom. But in fact, they wanted any information they could get out of me. They'd just kicked the Dutch out and here they were quizzing Johnny Cann from La Perouse, who knew nothing except where we'd been, and they were busily writing down everything I said—I couldn't get over that.

Then they asked me what the accommodation was like in Jayapura, the capital of Irian Barat and the biggest town on the north coast. They said King Leopold III of Belgium was coming to visit and they wanted to know where they could put him up.

'I've been in the top hotel in Jayapura, and it's pretty rough,' I said. 'I most certainly wouldn't recommend it for any royal people.' The last time I was there, I was friends with the missionaries and we stayed at their compounds, so I suggested they choose the best of them. 'They're high-class,' I said.

King Leopold was a keen amateur zoologist who even had an African snake named after him. Had I known that at the time, it might have set some alarm bells ringing. The Indonesians questioned me about all sorts of things and I told them about the animals we had and where we'd been and what the locals were like to deal with.

They seemed pretty happy with me so I asked them for a favour. My visa was for three months and it was about to run out. I had to leave the country to renew it. Was there any chance of bypassing that to save me the expense of the time lost before I went back into West New Guinea? They said no trouble, they'd make arrangements. I just had to go to LIPI's offices and it would all be sorted. But when I went back to LIPI and told them they said, 'We know nothing about that. You have 24 hours to leave the country and get a new visa or you'll be arrested.'

So I had to race back to Australia to renew my visa. And it was just as well that I did, because, typical of this expedition, people were saying one thing and doing another. For a start, I discovered that the Americans hadn't been sending my wages to Helen as agreed. She had no money and she had three little kids at the time and had to borrow off her mother who lived across the road. When Doug found out he blew up and Helen got all the back money immediately. She went from having nothing to more money than she knew what to do with. And my brother George was pleased that I was back—he got me to take over the snake show one Sunday to give him a break.

After I got my visa, I went straight back to New Guinea to help Doug finish the job. There were some specimens that we hadn't obtained yet, but I had to build crates and transportation cages for the others that were being kept in Irian Barat and, I thought, in Jakarta Zoo. When Doug and I returned to Port Moresby, we got some shocking news—none of the protected species had arrived at the American zoos. There were reptiles, small freshwater crocodiles, brolga cranes, rare long-beak echidnas, lizards and birds of paradise in the second shipment, and they were supposed to be looked after by the zoo. Doug jumped on a plane to Jakarta and asked the zoo's director where all the animals were.

'They died,' he said, implying it was our fault. Doug knew he was lying, something that was confirmed when he contacted the Bogor Museum. Our permits said that any animals that died in transit had to be sent to Bogor for examination. So Doug contacted Bogor and they said they'd received no animals from the zoo and they didn't know what Doug was talking about.

Needing to go further up the food chain, Doug went to see the Governor of Jakarta's secretary and discovered a pile of letters about us. Every village or town we went to, the Indonesian Governor in that village or town had to sign us up and let us stay there, so they had all those documents to show that we'd been authorised to be there and had permission to collect animals. They proved that everything we'd done was 100 per cent legal.

'I want to speak to the Governor,' Doug told the secretary. He said the Governor would see him for half an hour but it would cost $30,000. Doug just got up and walked out.

What happened then was a sadly typical tale of bureaucratic BS, bungling and—dare I say it—corruption. The zoo's director had been very helpful to begin with, encouraging us to bring our specimens back to his zoo because it was close to the airport. He had seen all our permits and knew we were fully approved to collect species for zoos.

But now he was being obstructive and evasive, even telling the authorities that we were poachers. It's a real shame and a missed opportunity, as American zoos can be very generous with their partners in foreign countries. It turned out we should have gone to Surabaya Zoo where the director, Mr Sigeto, was much more helpful (and didn't have a very high opinion of his Jakarta Zoo counterpart).

In the end, it was the animals that suffered and Doug's pride and joy, the echidna, lasted only another week after his last visit.

When we finally tracked down the missing animals, we discovered they had gone either to King Leopold III of Belgium, because he had connections with the Dutch, or had been sold in Germany and the Netherlands. The American zoos paid for the animals they did get, but that only just covered the cost of the expedition. Leon didn't make a cent. I was disappointed because we had been promised a big bonus for the birds of paradise, tree kangaroos, brolgas and other exotic animals.

That said, I was happy with the money and, truth be told, I would have done it for nothing—although I suspect Helen might have put her foot down.

CHAPTER 18

BACK TO WORK

WHEN WE RETURNED FROM NEW GUINEA, I WENT STRAIGHT BACK INTO CONSTRUC-tion work. I got a job with Woodall-Duckham, who were building the new waste-water treatment works in Malabar. I started there as a rigger and there was a big crew of workers there to begin with, but by the time the job was done I was the last man standing. All the bosses and workers had finished up and there was just me and the head man, Harry Steele.

For the last few weeks, Harry had me doing repairs on the defects the Water Board wanted fixed before the handover of the plant. If I could, I did the job myself, and if not I had to get tradies in or get replacements for the equipment that wasn't out of warranty. Towards the end of the contract, the Water Board sent inspectors in from all over Sydney to check every bolt, nail and screw in the plant. Clearly, they were going to hit us with a long list of repairs and replacement orders before the contract was finalised.

One of the last jobs that I was doing was the butterfly valves—monstrous valves more than a metre in diameter. The problem was that the locking bolts were moving when the valves were turned. It cost a lot of money and a lot of time, as we had to get the old bolts out and replace them with newer ones and we were having a tremendous amount of trouble. I got them as good as I could, but I couldn't get them to the prescribed pressure on the tension wrench without them slipping. The bolts really needed to be removed, roughened up and sealed with epoxy resin—but we didn't have time.

Harry Steele and the Water Board inspectors from Warragamba were all watching me as I tightened the bolts for the last time, but they still slipped. I'm pulling it back, pulling again, pull again, and I sneakily flicked the button off and it went 'Click, click, click, click'. The two inspectors said, 'Oh, beauty. That's good, John. Terrific.' But there was no sign of Harry—he couldn't watch and he'd walked away.

'That scared the Christ out of me,' he said when I caught up with him later. 'You've done well.'

In the last few days, the inspectors were all there with their charts, writing down crazy things they said had to be repaired. We had to replace hundreds of fluorescent tubes, which was a lot harder than it sounds. They were in flameproof cages and we had to build scaffolds to get to them then take them apart.

I pulled in a couple of my Koori mates to help. Meanwhile, the inspectors were working away, going for every bit of machinery and anything else that caught their eye. One wall that had some black marks on it—they demanded it be repainted.

The last day was coming and all the Water Board inspectors were grinning. They were all mates by then and they were laughing about all the things they'd found. Harry wasn't laughing. These blokes were going to hit us with a make-good demand that could bankrupt the company. It wasn't Harry's fault. With all the strikes that went on at the construction site, there was never a full day's work. Whenever the races were on or the water was good for diving or fishing, it was 'everybody out'.

The night before the hammer was due to come down and they would present us with their list of demands, Harry rang me up.

'John, come out and see me now,' he said. He was living near North Head, so I said it was a bit late to be travelling across Sydney.

'Don't worry,' he said. 'Come now.'

So I drove over there and as he opened the door his hands were shaking.

'Okay, what's up?' I said.

'Keep this to yourself,' he said. 'The contract expires at seven o'clock in the morning—not at the end of the day.'

It took a second to sink in, but that meant if they hadn't presented their demands by 7 a.m., they'd missed their chance. He handed me an envelope.

'Take this to work tomorrow and as soon as they show up, as long as it's after seven, give it to them,' Harry said.

The next morning, all the inspectors were there grinning, with all their charts and their notebooks. Right on seven o'clock out comes Jim, the head inspector, with two of his engineers.

'Okay, John,' he said. 'We've got some paperwork for you.'

'Have a look at this letter first, Jim,' I said.

Jim opened it and his jaw dropped. He read it and re-read it and then just stared at it and me. Finally, he spun around and marched to his office and said to the two engineers, 'Come with me.'

Everyone was standing around. 'What's going on, John?' one of them asked.

'See you, fellas, the party's over,' I said as I walked away. 'The contract is finished.'

Later that day I went up to the office the company had hired at Long Bay. Everyone had gone and Harry was there alone with a big grin on his face.

'My phone's been busy,' he said. 'It's all over. Done and dusted.'

I'd been selling off bits of plant and equipment as we scaled back on the work, and I asked him what he was going to do with the last ute we'd been running around in.

'Give me an honourable figure, John.'

I made an offer that was probably a lot less than honourable for a good Holden ute that was only three years old.

'It's yours,' he said.

I sold it a week later; that was my bonus.

All my mates were having a couple of weeks off when they'd finished, and I thought that would do for me too. I've never been on the dole in my life and I've hardly ever had a holiday, so I was making arrangements with one of my best mates to go diving somewhere when the phone rang.

'John,' a voice said, 'we need a crane driver at Kurnell.' That was the end of my holiday plans.

I wanted to get a job as a professional diver working underwater on the container wharf at Botany but there were no positions vacant. Instead they took me on as a diver's assistant with my mate Trevor Allen. Luckily—well, for some—there was a high turnover. There was another bloke before me and then the next guy committed suicide . . .

My longest full-time job was as a rigger with ICI. I was with them for nearly twenty years and they understood that I needed to go occasionally to search for turtles and attend conferences and the like. I suppose having someone like me on board—and providing me with support whenever they could—offset some of the criticisms they faced about what chemicals companies were doing to the environment. Whatever it was, it worked for me.

Wherever I was, and whatever I was doing, there were always my snakes and, increasingly, turtles, which were gradually becoming a bigger and bigger part of my life.

CHAPTER 19

TURTLE WARS

I WAS ASKED RECENTLY HOW DOES A SNAKEY, SPORTSMAN AND CONSTRUCTION worker become a world expert in turtles? Am I? I suppose I might be. I've written nine books on snakes and turtles, identified about a dozen new turtle species, travelled Australia and the world to lecture on turtles and historical matters related to reptiles, and helped various state museums to identify their specimens and catalogue their collections. I was also an honorary consultant to Queensland Museum and an advisor to the Tortoise and Turtle Group of the International Union of Conservation of Nature Survival Commission.

On top of that, I've received an Order of Australia, partly for my work with turtles and conservation generally, so I suppose I have to reluctantly admit that makes me something of an authority. The short answer to how this happened is that curiosity evolved into an interest and from there to what some people, my family included, would call an obsession.

Whenever I saw something swimming around when I was diving, I just became curious. I asked a lot of questions (my family say I still ask too many questions) but really I was asking myself. There are many unanswered questions when it comes to the wildlife of the rivers and saltwater habitats.

A few years back, for example, my main diving companion Harry Murphy and I were spearing at Pussycat Bay, just off the NSW Golf Club near Cape Banks. We were in about 10 metres of clear water, near where the SS *Minmi* was wrecked back in 1937.

A school of kingfish began to circle us and Harry hit the first one. They were all about the same size—1 metre. The speared fish broke off and Harry went to retrieve it, but I stopped him as the school was still swimming nearby and the wounded one was going nowhere and was just flapping on its side on the bottom. Unfortunately, the school headed away, so Harry dived to get the injured fish. But before he could get to it, another fish nosed under his mate and lifted it. Another one came to the other side and stopped it falling back, and its two helpers began to bump it out into deeper water and away they went, with Harry chasing in vain.

When he came up and got his breath, he immediately said, 'Did you see that?' I still do, 40 years later.

One of the most unusual and spectacular sights I've seen while river-diving occurred on 31 October 1990 in the Bellinger

River. About 5 kilometres upstream from Thora, I was drifting downstream in slow-flowing, clear water about 2 metres deep. There was a large, fallen log buried in river sand that extended to the bank.

Lined up along the log and at right angles to it, were about a dozen eels around 1–1.2 metres long. Their bodies lay quite straight and parallel to each other about 15–30 cm apart. Their heads were also almost in a straight line, and they appeared to be looking down into a deeper hole on the downstream side.

This hole had been formed when the river flowed at a faster rate, banking up gravel against the tree and swirling other soil away downstream. I held back rather than approach too close, and after watching for a few minutes, swam wide around them then slowly back upstream. From 5 metres, about the extent of good visibility there, I could see some activity in the darkness of the hole into which the eels were staring intently.

Diving slowly towards the sediment-darkened hole, I could see about another dozen similar-sized eels all swimming quickly around in the hole in an area of about 2 metres, the others watching from about 1.5 metres above. None of the eels seemed to pay any attention to me as I swam along the bottom close enough to notice two *Elseya* turtles lying apparently uninterested below them. I backed off and, on surfacing, continued downstream, marvelling at what I had seen.

I was always curious about how things work in the natural world. Why, for instance, why do some forms of abalone have great growths and parasites on their shells while others don't? I also noticed this when I was diving in New Zealand: the paua (blackfoot) had the growths on them, yet the yellowfoot at the same locations were always clear. Why?

Do some forms prevent this with a chemical, and if so might there be some application in anti-fouling treatments for boats? I have mentioned this a few times to marine biologists over the past 40 years and it sounds like they are finally taking an interest—or maybe they started asking the question themselves.

I see strange things all the time. Once, in the Gregory River in North Queensland, 100 kilometres upstream from the coast, a bull shark swam right up to me. It was steady, then his whole body started trembling with his eye almost poking out. When I told my mate Alex and asked him what he thought the trembling was all about, he said, 'He was only mimicking you.'

When I first became interested in turtles, there was virtually no research going on and no one knew too much about them. But I was a keen hobbyist and that's the real difference. Professionals do a university course and study biology and they'd go in any one of many fields. It's a job for them. They develop an interest and some of them get very keen but usually it starts off as their profession.

I developed an interest and then tried to study the science. To begin with, I got a book out of the library and learned the Latin names—well, the names of the turtles that had been identified. Then I started buying books, and before I knew it, I was crosschecking the information and thinking, 'Hey, this doesn't add up. This thing isn't what they're saying it is.'

So suddenly I had a couple of mysteries on my hands, which just made me more determined to find out the facts. At that point I started asking the experts for their advice and opinions and took it from there. I had a very good friend called Raymond Mascord who used to be a snake man but later became a top spider man. When he was doing his first book on spiders, Ray said to me casually that I'd probably never write a book on turtles.

I suppose the old competitive instinct kicked in, because I immediately thought, 'Oh, yes I will.' That's how I did the first one. And then I made friends with John Goode, the king of turtles in Australia and the author of *Freshwater Tortoises of Australia and New Guinea*. He was a journalist and wrote a lot of beautiful books, but what fired me up was that he was an amateur naturalist too.

When I did my first major turtle book in 1978, I showed it to Professor John Legler, who opened it up, flicked through two or three pages, saw a picture of himself and closed the book up.

'Oh yes,' he said in a snobby way. 'That'll serve its purpose.' Shortly after that he told me, 'I'd like to restrict your writing on turtles to only how to catch them and look after them in captivity.'

'Yeah, fair enough, John,' I said, but I took it as a pretty heavy insult, and assumed it was because he was an academic and I was an amateur. But I was wrong. Down the track, I told a good mate of mine, Dr Arthur Georges at the University of Canberra, about what Professor Legler had said.

'John Legler said something similar to me,' he said. 'He asked me if I'd please restrict my writing on turtles until he'd finished his own work.'

John died a few years ago and he'd still done nothing on Australian turtles, apart from the two that I found and he wrote up. You'd be surprised how competitive some zoologists can be. He just didn't want any opposition.

Since then I've published numerous magazine articles, two major turtle books—one of them in 2017—and my historical books: *Historical Snakeys* and *Snakes Alive*. The historical books are my favourites because while anyone could have written the turtle books over the years, I felt that I was the only one who could have written the books about the snakeys.

I had to do a lot of research, digging up the histories and finding photographs. I spent hours in the Mitchell and State libraries, and chasing people all over the world who had moved away. Most people wouldn't have known where to start. I lived in an era where all these old showman's families were dying and I missed talking to a lot of them, which hurt. A lot of it was my fault because I was too slow. There were boxes of pictures that were burnt and destroyed by families or relatives after the people had died. 'Who'd want them?' they thought. At least I saved this other stuff. That's there forever now.

I've also travelled a lot, mostly to the United States, giving talks on reptiles, snakes and turtles. I once went to New Zealand, where there are no tortoises, turtles or land snakes but I had a pretty strong following. The first meeting I went to, about snakes and reptiles, there were just the six of us: three guests, the two organisers and me. The second couldn't have been more different—it was held at a private zoo and there must have been 80 people there.

The crowds in America are usually pretty big because the reptile societies have large memberships. I've been both an 'also-ran' and top of the bill as a keynote speaker. There as here, there's a little bit of a division between the pros and the amateurs, although in one society there the pros and amateurs joined forces.

At one of the meetings in Orlando, Florida, there had been a hurricane a few days before and one of the top amateur turtle breeders in the world, a real conservationist, had suffered a lot of damage with all his pens and walls blown down. Luckily his house was missed, but there were trees across his roadway and a lot of damage to his turtle areas.

One of the boys suggested we go and give him a hand. I think nineteen of us were amateurs, and every one of us went down to his house to help him clear up and get everything back together. As far as I know none of the professionals went. No doubt people did have flights booked to go out straight after the conference, but it upset a lot of the amateurs. Ironically, this conference was partly intended to fix up all the differences between the amateurs and pros. These days it's all a bit more free and easy—amateurs are welcome at the professionals' meetings and vice versa.

After I'd been in Orlando, I got an invitation to dive and give a talk at the Nuclear Research Station on the Savannah River in South Carolina. It was an honour to be invited by Dr Witt-Gibbens, undoubtedly one of the top guys in his field. However, even with permits I had trouble getting through the gates—this was one of the highest security areas in the States. The meeting and the diving in the Savannah River went for a couple of days, but they took me off site to sleep in a motel and that was fair enough. The top brass knew I was no risk—when I took my golden handshake from ICI back in 1987, one of the managers told me I'd been checked out by the FBI. Just as well they never knew I once lived next door to a communist!

I have to say that over the years I have stirred up my fair share of controversy and there are a few people—both scientists and hobbyists—who disagree with me. All I can do is quote a mate of mine, Professor Gunther Thieschinger, who says: 'How can you conserve an environment when you don't know what is in it? Without identification and description you have a language without words.'

One of the problems is that, although some scientists make their living working on turtles, as far as I'm concerned they don't fully understand them. Some seem to wait for DNA results and then do the writing or descriptions.

So what is a species or subspecies? Who decides such things and when? Many scientists don't believe in classifying subspecies, but if populations are geographically isolated and distinctly different, both morphologically and biologically, but when brought together could still produce fertile offspring, then I believe they warrant their own status as subspecies, chiefly for conservation purposes.

There's danger inherent in accepting isolated facts without examining the wider context. Take the eastern snake-neck turtle (*Chelodina longicollis*), for example. A scientist found 300 specimens in the field and stated they were safe, but given that John Goode, Dr Col Limpus, Charles Tanner and I had previously found thousands of them, this 300 figure actually represented a dramatic decline in the population. Col Limpus says the species is virtually extinct in the Brisbane metropolitan area.

The evolutionary 'trees' for turtles constructed using DNA evidence have seen numerous changes over the last fifteen years and there are likely to be more in the coming years. Why? Because some scientists are relying almost solely on the genetic results to determine species divisions and relationships with very little reliance on other knowledge.

Using five different genes, one of the world's top DNA experts has stated that *Chelodina canni* and *C. rankini* are 2 per cent different, yet other scientists still maintain that they're the same species. Morphological differences within the saw-shell turtle (*Wollumbinia latisternum*) complex are tremendous, yet scientists relying on genetics alone continue to regard them as a single species.

There will be accepted changes in the future. The original species concept still used by some scientists says that the different turtles will not interbreed, but of course, they do. The northern long-neck turtle (now m. *Chelodina (macrochelodina) oblonga regosa*) and *C. canni* will naturally hybridise where they overlap, as will Georges' turtle (*Wollumbinia georgesi*) and a locally occurring or introduced species of *Emydura* in the Bellinger River, but they're still regarded as distinct species. While the information provided by DNA analysis is an advantage in many ways, it should be used in combination with morphological and biological characteristics.

Morphological and biological differences such as size, babies, number of eggs and eye colour are all important, and some morphological differences become more distinct in aged specimens or are best seen in hatchlings. Some scientists claim that most of the populations of *Emydura macquarii* in different river systems on the east coast are all the same, but in my view they're not. Based on the features of their morphology and biology, these warrant being treated as separate subspecies.

From a conservation point of view this is important, as some of these populations may be at risk and this is ignored while they're all viewed as identical. Four of the subspecies of

E. macquarii have been rejected by some—but these beautiful turtles need acceptance and protection.

The criticism from institution-based turtle researchers regarding the legitimacy of the species of turtles I have described has, in my opinion, not been justified. In describing new species or subspecies I have taken into consideration a range of characteristics that includes their morphology, biology and the extent to which they are isolated from other species—not just their genetic similarities or differences. The description of these new species is important for their conservation and, with the threats they face these days, far more than just an academic exercise. I think attitudes will change with the publication of my 2017 book (with Ross Sadlier), *Freshwater Turtles of Australia*.

I have mates for whom conservation and photography, rather than collecting, are the main focus these days and I've been up north with them four or five times. I fly to Cairns and then we take four-wheel drives up to the Gulf Country or the Cape.

For collecting, I've made a couple of major trips up in the last few years to Cape York with Origin Energy and my mate Alastair Freeman of Aquatic Threatened Species in the Queensland Department of Environment Protection and Heritage. He was interested in the endangered species and we were working on the flatback turtles with the local Aboriginals.

The biggest problem up there are the thousands and thousands of wild pigs digging up turtle nests and devastating the turtle population. One pig there kept digging eggs up and they could never catch him—he was too smart for them. When they finally shot him and opened him up, they found 30 or 40 dead baby flatback turtles in his belly.

Origin Energy are a bit on the nose with a lot of people in the conservation world, but I have to give it to them: they hired a helicopter and snipers and they shot hundreds of wild pigs over a couple of seasons.

Freshwater Turtles of Australia is the culmination of decades of interest in and study of turtles. I have thousands of turtle photographs to sort out, and many of them have never been mounted or even looked at, so I've handed them all on to Ross Sadlier. He has 2500 of my turtle photos on his computer already.

So, yes, maybe my family are right and my hobby did become an obsession.

CHAPTER 20

MY BROTHER GEORGE

MY BROTHER GEORGE MORRIS CANN WAS BORN IN JULY 1927 AT HILL 60, YARRA Bay. Soon after, our parents needed somewhere more substantial to live so they built a place on the hill. The only photograph I ever saw of the house was the large deep sand pit that had been built for snakes, with the house in the background. The houses and shacks are long gone from the hill. It was around 1936, after Noreen was born, that the family moved to better accommodation in the Customs Building at La Pa closer to the display pit for the snake show.

By the time I came along in 1938, George was eleven years old and was already travelling with Pop, whether it was for catching snakes or to help with shows. But the following year travelling to shows came to an end, when Pop accepted the position of curator of reptiles at Taronga Park Zoo. Opportunities expanded in another direction, however, when Pop persuaded the police to lift a ban on showing venomous reptiles, and showmen could ply their trade at the Sydney Royal Easter Show for the first time in many years.

Things were on the up for the Canns. In 1940 we moved to our current home in Yarra Bay and Pop built massive above-ground snake pits that could hold the 200 tiger snakes that Eric Worrell and Ken Slater collected to be milked for venom for the Commonwealth Serum Laboratories.

Because of the age difference, George and I never hunted snakes together when I was young, and I don't recall him hunting too much with Pop until he got older. I recall one time when George and I went to the Chinese Gardens at Botany, a few kilometres from where we lived, to catch golden bell frogs. They're now classified as an endangered species but at the time they were common. They were in water wells made from railway sleepers and there were dozens of them. One time George collected 100 and I caught about 60—these were Pop's food for the snakes in the pits.

After Pop bought his Ford ute, the three of us travelled to various places, such as Lake George, together. We always caught a few snakes on our one- or two-day trips, but we never ever took any home. It was just a good day's outing.

Sometimes we went together to the Barmah Swamps on the New South Wales banks of the Murray River. Once we were there the day before the duck season opened, and there was an occasional car passing on the bush tracks, obviously looking for a good shooting location. We were there sitting on a log having coffee, waiting for a bit of heat to bring out the tiger snakes, when a car with a few people in it went past us and stopped a bit further along around a corner. A few moments later, we heard an ear-splitting scream and I said, 'Come on, George. The snakes are out.' We went around the short bend and there was a lady climbing over the log and pulling up her dacks. I jumped over the log and sure enough grabbed the big nice-banded tiger. One of the crowd of people in the car said, 'How come you knew there was a snake there?'

George and I looked at each other. 'Why else would she be screaming?' I said.

In his younger days, George was extremely fit. We regularly had footraces around the blocks. Skipping was all the go in those days and I never did any, but George and his mates did and all they were pretty good, like the top boxers. In fact, a mob of them, George and his army mates, used to box at Woolloomooloo Police Boys' Club. George was a good boxer—a welterweight, I think—and whenever he went there he used to spar with Jimmy Carruthers, who would later be a bantamweight world champion. Les Dorry was the trainer and he also trained me, Les Davidson and Willo Longbottom, when we went there instead of our usual Kensington or Kingsford Police Boys' Clubs.

George had never had any intention of being either an amateur or professional fighter. He was just keeping fit. Somewhere kicking around I have a cup he was awarded when he won the army championship on HMAS *Kanimbla*, a cruise ship that had been converted into an armed troopship during World War II. Then he went to Japan and somewhere along the line he won another title, but that was it. He never fought again.

George was called up to the Australian Imperial Forces on 7 August 1945 and began his jungle training at Canungra, Queensland. He was in luck. The Japanese officially surrendered a week later (Germany had already surrendered a few months before). George's army days had a long way to go, however—he wasn't discharged until September 1948, and his service was listed as 351 days in Australia and 650 days overseas.

At various times he was stationed at Bougainville or Rabaul Prison hospitals as an orderly. While he was there a high-ranking Japanese officer in George's section committed suicide using a knife to cut his own throat. The Japanese officer still had his uniform on and George acquired all the ribbons that he'd been wearing. Years later, he showed them to me, with their black bloodstains still clearly visible.

Besides Bougainville and Japan, George was stationed in Germany and England. While in Germany during the occupation, George and a few mates went to visit a tourist town that had survived the Allies' bombs. The town was Hamelin, best known for the legend of the Pied Piper. The three diggers had a meal at the famous old restaurant pub, called the Rattenfängerhaus. George brought home the menu, which had nine pages of text and pictures relating to its history.

George did his snake displays at schools, shopping centres and showgrounds, as well as TV ads and film work. We collected snakes together all over the place, including on Flinders and Chappell islands in Tasmania, and at Lake George near Canberra. We had a competition every day for the first, the biggest and the most caught, with a prize of a beer for the winner of each category. The first snake caught was important because if the weather was bad and only one snake was caught, that was all three categories won and the loser had to buy the winner three beers.

George was bitten by snakes ten times. Once he was bitten by a brown snake at La Pa and they took him away in an ambulance. Someone came rushing over to my house to tell me and luckily I was home, so I whipped up to the hospital and went straight into the emergency room. I knew where it was—I think I might have been in there once or twice myself. I walked in and George had a pressure bandage on his arm, which was then the new treatment, with a nurse and a sister watching him.

'How are you?' I asked.

'Oh, no trouble at all,' he said. 'I don't even remember passing out.'

'No antivenom?' I said.

'No, not at this stage,' he said. 'I don't think I need it.'

In came the doctor and said to the sister: 'I think it's been an hour now. You can take the pressure bandage off.'

'Hang on, Doc,' I said. 'Don't take that pressure bandage off. You've got to have antivenom on standby if they're going to take the pressure bandage off.'

'Don't tell me how to do my job,' he said.

'I'm telling you,' I said. 'You don't take it off without having antivenom on hand, just in case.'

'Get out or I'll call security,' he said.

'Okay,' I said. 'But I've warned you.'

As I was walking out the door I heard the sister say, 'Doctor, he knows what he's talking about. You need the antivenom.' As I was sitting outside I saw one of the sisters come past with the antivenom out of the fridge, just in case. But they didn't need it. They kept George there for another couple of hours before I took him home.

George survived the snakebite but he wasn't immune. He'd have needed to take several small bites regularly over a long period for any resistance to develop. Graeme Gow, our mate from the Top End, was bitten a lot and he reckoned he was immune from snakebite, but when Dr Struan Sutherland checked his blood, he said he had no resistance in his system at all. He survived a lot of bites, but on at least one occasion he was in trouble and needed antivenom.

Before George retired at 65, he worked as a plumber and fitter for Wormald Brothers who were a fire protection firm. One of George's jobs was to go each fortnight to the James Hardie factory and dust the asbestos off the fire valves and pipes in the ceiling. There's no doubt that dust led to him contracting mesothelioma.

George died on my birthday, on 15 January 2001. Some people think I'm heartless when I say it was the best birthday present I ever had, but then they probably never had to watch someone they care about dying a slow and horrible death like that, literally fighting for every breath.

Voice of the bush—a tribute to George Cann

by Neville Burns (extract)

Well, I got the news this morning, mate, that you had
gone away
The tears were running freely, I'm not afraid to say.
But we were blessed to know you, George, though we are
now apart
And the many things that made you special now live on in
our hearts.

The humour, kindness and mateship that you showed
to everyone
Were known throughout the country, mate, and now your race
is run.
A part of Aussie tradition goes with you, we all know.
The last of the travelling snake men, who lived to do his show.

A man known by sight to thousands who visited 'The Loop'
On a Sunday afternoon at La Perouse, you'd always find
a group
Of people gathered round 'The Pit' to watch the snake man
with snow-white hair.
Yes, there will be many who'll miss you, mate, now you can't
be there.

The Cann family tradition that has been around so long
Started by your Dad many years ago, and carried on by you
   and John,
A tradition you were proud of mate, and so glad to be a part
A symbol of the love for your Dad that you carried in
   your heart.

I wonder how many people knew, George, that in your pocket
   at each show
You always tucked a piece of cord, used by your Dad all those
   years ago
A very moving gesture, of love and deep respect
A bond that sadly in this world so many would neglect.

With a lively sense of humour, strong in the way a man
   should be,
To many a younger man and inspiration, as you surely were
   to me.
If a mate was feeling badly, they could count on Georgie Cann
He'd always be the first to lend a helping hand.

And now you're gone from us but our memories will never
   cease
We just want to say George, dear old mate, rest in peace.

CHAPTER 21

MY FAMILY

AS YOU KNOW, I FIRST NOTICED HELEN WHEN I WAS WORKING AT THE HOSPITAL just before the 1956 Olympics and she worked on the big ironing press in the laundry. I noticed a really good-looking sort and in disbelief my boss pointed out that she lived across the road from me.

I had no idea. Her father was a blacksmith and he and his wife had come to Yarra Bay from the scrub in the north-west of New South Wales in a horse and covered wagon years before. Helen had seven sisters and two brothers and they lived 45 degrees across the road. But my mates and I ran our own race— spearfishing and the like—and she and her sisters did their own thing, so we never met properly until I was eighteen.

I'd known her for a few years before we ever went out, but as time went on I started seeing a little bit more of her. We used to go out dancing but I never danced much. She was keen but

I was no good. I could only do the La Perouse free step—go wherever you want to.

Sometimes there was a La Perouse Football Club event or turnout, and other times we'd meet up with Ali Ardler and his wife, who used to drink at the old Bat and Ball Hotel in Redfern. They were a great old Aboriginal couple, and a crowd of us locals just seemed to join them even though it was a fair way from our district. And all the mob danced. I knew this hotel well from my athletics days—the athletes named it the Kensington Arms, and all the old pros used to have a beer there after training. As time went on, I suppose you would say Helen and I were going steady—at least when I was in town. It must have been frustrating for her, waiting for me to come back from wherever I was working, then spend a few days together before I was off again.

Once we'd decided to get married, I thought I should get us a house, so I went for a loan to build on the land I'd bought with my motorbike money. First I went to the Commonwealth Bank, because like every schoolkid I'd put my money into the Commonwealth and that's where I had my account. I never had much money in the bank—just a few hundred quid.

'What sort of collateral have you got?' the bloke asked.

'Well, I own a block of land next door,' I said. He said it wasn't enough and told me he couldn't help me.

So I came out and I walked across the road to the National Bank of Australia and asked to see the manager. He called me over and I told him I was looking for a loan.

'John Cann?' he said. 'You're a footballer, aren't you?'

'Well, I *was* a footballer, yes,' I said.

We had a yarn about football and then he asked me what I wanted and gave me the loan. I borrowed the princely sum of 2750 pounds and, when currency was decimalised, our payments were $37.50. We did it hard at times but we never missed a payment. The house that we built back then is the same one we're sitting in today, 50-odd years later.

The wedding was a simple affair. We got married at the Catholic church at Malabar and our families booked the hall at Matraville (now the library), did all the catering and put in a couple of kegs of beer. We went back to the hall for the reception and speeches and all that. We didn't have a band but we had a record player and there was a fair bit of dancing going on.

Helen and I went home to change into our party clothes. But by the time we got back, the families had parked the touring caravan a mate had lent us for our honeymoon outside and they just herded us into it. The next thing we knew they were waving us goodbye before they went back inside to whoop it up. They didn't want us drinking before we drove off on the honeymoon.

Helen wasn't much of an outdoors person, and she never liked snakes—still doesn't. She'd wanted to go to the Gold Coast as she'd never been there. I told her it was too hot up there in March so we went down the south coast. Back then, every holiday I got, I would go snaking, and later on hunting for turtles.

We headed south and I went spearfishing down near Bega and then went down to Eden where we stayed in a caravan park. Further down the track outside Lakes Entrance in Victoria we got stopped by a fruit inspector who refused to believe the tomatoes we had with us had been bought locally. He told us if we moved the caravan he'd call the police. So I asked him if I could eat them there and he said yes. Then he told me to move the caravan because it was blocking the road in front of his little hut. I reminded him he'd threatened to call the police if we moved it, and I made him wait until Helen had cooked the tomatoes and I'd eaten them. We'd both just had breakfast and Helen wasn't hungry but she saw a side of me that morning that she'd never seen before. Lesson learned—keep your grocery receipts when you're on the road.

We moved on down to just outside Melbourne and went to visit old Charlie Tanner, a great old snake man and a good mate. We spent a few days with him and looked at all his snakes, and went around to Portsea where Harold Holt drowned (or according to some idiot was taken by Chinese submarines). I went spearfishing inside the heads there, which was interesting.

A bloke came out in a rowing boat and asked if I could help him.

'Mate, can you dive for my traps?' he said. 'The boats have smashed the glass floats I had on them.'

I said fair enough—it was no skin off my nose and I thought we might score a free lobster or something. Down I went and had a look around, and sure enough I found a trap—a bloody big hook with a big bit of meat on it.

'What are you catching?' I said when I handed him the rope.

'Sharks,' he said. 'There's plenty of them here.'

That was the only trap I got for him.

On the way back we went to Lake George, where I caught all those tiger snakes I mentioned earlier. We met my mate Sylvester Smith on his property and I asked him the best place to put the caravan.

'Follow my tractor down,' he said. 'You'll get bogged anywhere else.'

So down we went and then he pulled up in his tractor and waited for me around the front.

'Where do you keep your snake bags, John?' he asked.

'In the caravan,' I said. 'Why?'

'Better get them out. You've parked your caravan right over a big tiger snake.'

Helen wasn't too impressed.

Later we went snaking and I was getting a fair few tiger snakes. Helen was petrified and it was a stinking hot day, so she went back to the caravan and Sylvester went home and left me to it.

The tiger snakes were pretty lively in the heat, and one came up and scratched some blood across my knuckle. I sucked a bit of venom from around the wound. They reckon that does no good but I figure that if it's not sitting there, it's not going to soak into you. On my way back to the van I walked past a number of tiger snakes still lying out in the heat, but I wasn't going to take any more chances. It was the only time I was ever scared of snakes. I didn't know whether I was going to be affected by the bite, so I got back to the caravan and we stayed there overnight and I felt okay. That was the end of the snaking part of the honeymoon, much to Helen's relief.

Helen gave up working at the laundry when she was pregnant with Paul. He was born on 17 July 1965. Jace was born on 7 December 1966, the anniversary of Pearl Harbor. His name was John but we called him JC and then it became Jace and everyone thinks that's his name now. If someone called him John, he wouldn't know what they were talking about.

Belinda came along on 28 April 1972. Her nickname is Bindi, which we got off Belinda 'Bindi' Sutton, who used to live next door to us and these days is best known as the aunty of John Sutton, the first-grade footballer for South Sydney. And it's from her, indirectly, that Bindi Irwin got her name.

Her late father Steve was just getting going as a TV zoologist and he'd dropped in to film me and my snakes. We were down the backyard, and there was Steve and his manager–cameraman and me. My daughter Belinda came out and I said, 'Hey, Bindi, we've finished filming here. How about putting a coffee on?'

'Bindi?' Steve said. 'Where did you get the name Bindi from? I've never heard that before.'

I said her real name was Belinda but we all called her Bindi because we got the name off the little Aboriginal girl next door. So, next thing we hear, he had a dog and then a crocodile and finally a daughter called Bindi. A few years later they asked him in an interview where he got the name Bindi.

'Oh, I got it off a little Aboriginal girl in Cape York,' he said. I suppose that sounded better than a little Aboriginal girl from La Perouse.

None of my kids are interested in snakes, but Paul and Jace both got my athletics genes. Paul held the New South Wales age discus record until Jace took it off him when he beat the Australian age-group record distance by a third—a mark that stood for 22 years. I guess we're all genetically suited to athletics. I never lifted a weight or set foot in a gym (until I took up boxing). People who've seen pictures of me competing at sixteen find that hard to believe but it's true.

When Jace was a couple of years out of Little Athletics and in Year 10, I was informed that the Athletics Association of New South Wales was running a state competition, with the winners to be selected to compete in the Australian school championships in Hobart. I asked, with an effort, if Jace wanted to have a try-out in the competition. Up to that point he'd never done any weight-training, unlike many other kids, because I believed young kids shouldn't lift weights.

But now he was fifteen and ready to compete at state level I changed my mind and took him to the sports gym that had recently been set up at Matraville near Yarra Bay. Jace had done a few bench presses when a bloke came up to me.

'Is that your son?' he asked.

'Yup.'

'He's a bit rough round the edges,' he said. 'Where does he train?'

'He doesn't,' I said. 'This is the first time he's set foot in a gym.'

The bloke looked at me like I was mad or having a lend.

'I'd like to train him in weightlifting,' he said. 'There's probably only one kid in the state who lifts heavier weights than him. With a bit of training he could go a long way.'

So I asked Jace if he fancied training as a weightlifter.

'Not interested,' was all he said.

The next day there was a knock on the door. The same bloke had tracked us down.

'Look,' he said. 'Your boy has so much raw talent, and I guarantee that in three months he'll be competing in Asia. He's a one-off.'

So I asked Jace again but got the same response: 'Not interested.'

Helen agreed—she didn't want him getting into weightlifting.

History repeats. A few months later we turned up for the junior athletics trials for the state team to go to Tasmania—the scene of my first interstate athletics comp. But when we got there, we noticed Jace's name wasn't on the program.

THE LAST SNAKE MAN

So we went to the officials' tent, where there were a few parents and kids with the same question. The officials told us they didn't have a green slip for Jace from his school, and if you didn't have a green slip you couldn't compete.

'What's a green slip?' I asked.

'It's a permission slip that has to be signed by both a parent and a teacher,' this bloke says.

'Well, I'm his parent,' I said, 'and his teacher's standing right over there so give us a slip and we'll sign it.'

'Nope,' said this jumped-up paper shuffler. 'We're organising this on a professional basis and we can't have people just wandering in off the street wanting to take part.'

We weren't the worst off—families who'd travelled from Broken Hill and Tweed Heads were also rejected for not having their green slips.

'God,' I said. 'You bastards never change. You stuffed athletics for me when I was a kid and you're still stuffing it up now with your bureaucratic bullshit.

'Come on, son,' I said to Jace. 'Let's go and get your surfboard.'

At the age of 50 he still surfs and goes spearfishing—and at the time of writing we'll be eating lobster for the second night in a row.

Helen didn't go back to work again until I got the turtle bug, chasing them all over Australia. It was taking up a lot of my time and it was costing a lot of money, so she said, 'I'll go back for a year and you can spend more time running after turtles.'

So she went back to work for a year . . . and ten years later she retired. She was a very good press hand and got her old job back straight away—she even qualified again for superannuation.

And even though she wasn't outdoorsy, as I said, she came with me on some long trips and never complained. She doesn't go in the water, but she'd look out for crocodiles and cook our meals and hold the turtles while I was photographing them. One time, back in 1990, I got my long service leave and we travelled around Australia for three months looking for turtles. Every week or so we might go into a caravan park where she'd have a proper shower with hot water—otherwise it was a camp shower in the bush.

I had a big box trailer to carry all our gear and put the boat on top. To keep the gear down I had those camping mattresses that roll up and then self-inflate to two-inches deep when you open them out. I wouldn't sleep on one now, but Helen stuck it out for three months. It was only years later when the family was chatting about not being able to sleep or the toughest trip they'd been on or something like that she let on how bad it was.

'The worst trip of my life trying to sleep on those mongrel mattresses,' Helen said, out of the blue.

'What are you talking about?' I said. 'You never complained.'

'What was the sense in complaining?' she said.

Which reminds me of the Coolgardie cooler (or safe, as it was often called) that Pop had made at Hill 60 at Yarra, before the days when everybody had fridges, or even electricity to run them. The Coolgardie cooler was basically a box with hessian walls that sat in a tray of water with some felt, if you had it. The water would get drawn up into the hessian, where it would evaporate (especially if there was a breeze) and that would cool the air inside the box. It would get pretty cold inside and last a day or so before you had to top up the water.

Years before this trip with Helen, when I was working on turtles with Professor John Legler, he would use my place as a launching pad. We went bush a few times in his Land Rover station wagon but he never took ice with him, which annoyed me because I like my beer cold. He did have a roll of cheesecloth, which he used to soak in water then use to store the turtles for transportation back to base in the back of the wagon. It worked pretty well.

One day I got some of his cheesecloth and I put a few beers in it, tied the corners, dipped it in the river and hung it up in a tree where it could catch a bit of a breeze.

'What are you doing that for?' he asked, so I explained that it was a Coolgardie cooler and how it worked.

'That's bullshit,' he said. 'That beer will just get warmer.'

I let it go at that. The cheesecloth dried out after a while so I re-wet it and stuck it back up. Later on, John was cooking with his shirt off, just his shorts on. I pulled a beer out of the bag and stuck it on his back. He screamed like a stuck pig. He couldn't believe how cold the beer had got in that cheesecloth. That's how a Coolgardie cooler worked and I used it a few times before we got Eskies and suchlike.

Helen and I went right around Australia on that trip, starting in Sydney, south through Victoria, over to Adelaide, up to Port Augusta and then straight across the Nullarbor to Western Australia. Then we went up to the Kimberleys and along the Gibb River Road to Darwin, across the Top End and back down through Queensland.

We weren't collecting—we were taking measurements and photographing a lot of turtles. Poor Helen. We'd find a beautiful spot and she'd have her deckchairs out while I was diving. But then bingo, I'd have my turtle and my photographs and I'd be ready to go.

'Oh no, I want to stay here for a couple of days,' she'd say, but I'd tell her we had to go. I had a timetable.

For three months we camped every night and lit a fire and did our own cooking. Later on she showed me a film she'd made on the trip. I didn't realise until then that she was shit-scared every time I went diving because in some places there were a lot of crocs around.

One day we went to Sara Henderson's property, Bullo River Station. When I asked her for permission to dive, she said I could dive in the river but I had to be careful and not cross the causeway the army had built for her.

'Don't go downstream from that crossing because it's full of crocodiles,' she said. 'Upstream is okay—that's where our workhands wash.'

So that's where I dived, even though I wasn't 100 per cent convinced the crocodiles couldn't walk across a road. It was a great dive because I got what I was really after. There were two species of turtle in this river system that I really needed to find and photograph. Both had been collected and described from this waterway back in the 1800s.

But the water was murky and dirty, with pandanus all around, so as soon as I got the second one I was looking for I got out. I snuck back to our camp and that's when I saw Helen shooting the video, but I couldn't hear what she was saying. I found out when we got home and she played it back.

'John's been gone a long time,' she said. 'There's a lot of crocodiles here and I'm really, really worried about where he is.'

I've got to give it to her: she put up with the flies and the heat and the campsites and cooking on an open fire. A couple of years later I would get the Order of Australia for my contributions to turtle research, conservation, the environment and the community, but it was Helen who deserved a medal.

CHAPTER 22
MARTIN LAUER

THE DAY WE GOT BACK FROM OUR THREE-MONTH EXPEDITION AROUND AUSTRALIA, I had a phone call out of the blue from Germany. It was Martin Lauer—we hadn't spoken since we became good mates at the 1956 Olympics in Melbourne.

Like me, Martin was a decathlete. Being a little older—and possibly having had better training—he was very generous with his time and advice when we met at the Olympics. He was a bit better, too, coming fifth representing West Germany, and won bronze in his specialty event, the 110-metre hurdles.

Martin was phoning to check I'd got a letter he'd sent about a planned trip to Australia, specifically the Kimberleys. My brother George hadn't had a chance to pass it on to us, though, so this was the first I'd heard about it. I told him he was welcome to stay with us in Yarra Road. Martin accepted the invitation, and suggested we come with him and his wife Christa on the trip.

'Mate,' I said, 'we just got back from there.'

I wondered if he appreciated the distances and I thought his timing was slightly out given the coming wet season, when some roads become unusable. Another problem was that he wanted to tackle the Red Centre. They were coming from Europe, which was cold but had proper roads everywhere, to a huge area where many of the roads were just dirt tracks.

I was worried for him and Christa. Did they know what they were getting into? Did they realise it could take a week to drive from the Kimberleys to Sydney? I needn't have worried. Martin fell in love with the outback and even spent an extra day at William Creek, near Lake Eyre in South Australia. On New Year's Eve he met and became mates with a crusty old bloke who called himself 'Joe the dingo hunter', who had no teeth and was out of work. Maybe there was a dingo shortage.

But what had happened in the intervening years? And why had Martin never replied to the letters I sent him when I was laid up with my broken neck? Martin had carried on with athletics, and at the 1958 European Championships he won the gold in 110-metre hurdles. That year he ran his first world record, in the 4 x 100-metre relay, and the next year he broke the world record in the 110-metre hurdles, which stood until 1972. He also set his personal best in the decathlon and was ranked second in the world. He was the first person to be voted Athlete of the

Year in the inaugural edition of the sports magazine *Track & Field News*.

Martin ran the anchor leg for West Germany's 4 x 100-metre relay team that won gold at the 1960 Rome Olympics after the United States team was disqualified for an incorrect baton change. Martin was forced to retire shortly thereafter when a non-sterile injection went bad and he was facing the prospect of losing a leg.

It turned out, while I was lying in hospital after breaking my neck, he was in hospital too, telling his doctors there was no way they were cutting off his leg. He still has trouble with it now. It got worse for Martin; on her way to visit him in hospital, his girlfriend was killed in a car crash, and his brother died several years later from the injuries he sustained in the same accident.

After recovering, Martin took up sailing and failed by only a few seconds to qualify for the Olympics. Then, amazingly, he became a country and western singer—cowboy hat, the lot—recording albums with the songs in German on one side and English on the other. Someone liked them—he sold millions. About ten years after their trip to Australia, Martin paid for Helen and me to fly to Germany—proof, if any were needed, that his determination, intelligence and competitive spirit had paid off for him, big time.

In his collection of memorabilia, he had an Australian athlete's track singlet and he didn't know who it belonged to, although he suspected it might have been Peter Hatfield's. Peter competed for Australia in the decathlon in the 1960 Olympics and Martin wanted me bring it back to Australia and return it to him. The thing was, I recognised the number—it was mine, although I didn't let on. After a few beers one day we had a mini-decathlon in his backyard and I wore my singlet (which seemed to have shrunk over the years).

While we were there Knut Tasker told me he was writing a book about Martin and asken me if I'd like to contribute something. Not long after we got home, Knut phoned and asked me to send the piece to him but not tell Martin what I was doing. In it, I told the story of how we'd met and reconnected years later, and revealed for the first time who that singlet really belonged to.

A few months later I got a parcel from Germany containing a signed copy of the book. In the dedication, Martin had written, 'Hi mate, am I the mug now?'

*　*　*

That phone call out of the blue was the start of a friendship that lasts to this day. Helen and I have travelled many times with Martin and Christa, both here and in Europe. And during the Sydney Olympics, he brought a steady stream of visiting athletes out to Yarra Road to enjoy some good old-fashioned Australian hospitality. Remarkably, Martin calls me at 4 p.m. every day, just to say hi and check that I'm okay. More than 50 years after the event, our friendship is as strong as ever.

On one of our trips to Germany in 2009, Martin and Christa took Helen and me to that same restaurant in Hamelin George had visited with his army mates back in the 1940s. We arrived in Hamelin on a charter boat that Martin skippered on the Weser River for a week. I'd brought George's 50-year-old menu with me and I was pleasantly surprised when I saw a display case at the entrance with artefacts and a history of the place. The menu would have fitted right in there.

The waitress sat us down in the very alcove depicted on page four of the old menu, and we were given a new menu, which was just as impressive. Martin told the waitress in German that we'd like to speak to the manager. We were going to show him the old menu. She returned and said that he was busy but he'd come to see us shortly. During our meal and drinks over the next two hours, Martin asked twice more, but the manager never came. So we left with the old menu and a copy of the new one, and they missed out on seeing a bit of their own history.

One trip in Germany was an adventure of a different kind. We flew into Frankfurt and then had to catch a train to Milan, where Martin was waiting for us. His daughter met us and put us on the train, where we got into a compartment with a nice-looking young woman. Before we left, Martin's daughter spoke to her in German (although it turned out she spoke perfect English, with a slight American accent). We had to change trains in Mannheim for a connection through Switzerland to Italy.

It was one of those compartment trains with the corridor down one side and sliding doors opening to two bench seats facing each other. I was exhausted from the flight so I stretched out on one seat and slept while Helen and the young woman chatted away. The next thing I knew, Helen and the girl were shaking me: 'Wake up! Wake up!' Helen said. 'This is where we get off.'

So we grabbed our bags and crossed the platform to the other train and settled down for the long part of the journey. Eventually, a bloke in uniform came in and asked to see our passports. That seemed odd, given we were still in Germany, but whatever . . . I felt in my pocket. No passport. I told Helen she must have the passports and she checked in her bag for the big travel wallet that had our passports, plane tickets and $5000 in cash in it. Gone! The nice girl who was so helpful had robbed us. In fact, as soon as I dozed off, first chance she got she must have sprayed Helen with gas to make her sleep too.

The railway police came in and we described everything that had happened and they just nodded, like they knew it already (which I suppose they did). Helen was able to give them a detailed description of the woman and they phoned head to get the train searched at the next station while we got off the Milan train and waited. After a couple of hours a German copper arrived on a train going back the other way.

'She must have liked you,' he said. 'We found your wallet in the toilet. Normally they just throw it out of the window.'

Sure enough, the tickets and passports were all there, but the money was gone. The girl had struck gold with us. At least now we could continue our journey, several hours late and with no money. We searched our pockets for any spare cash we might have but all I could find was one $5 note. I had to push my way—politely—to the front of the bureau de change queue just to change one lousy fiver before the next train went. But at least it got us a cup of tea and a sandwich to share.

Martin had been alerted at this stage and his daughter, who worked high up in a bank, arranged for more cash to be waiting for us in Milan. Luckily, I'd just sold a lot of pictures to an author who was writing a book about turtles, so we were able to get the money transferred and we had a couple of thousand dollars to spend.

Martin had hired a cabin cruiser in Venice, so we spent a wonderful time there and soon forgot about our ordeal on the train . . . almost. We were lucky—our friendship with Martin and Christa restored our faith in human nature, which had been so cruelly shattered. And, hey, isn't that what friends are for?

CHAPTER 23

REPTILES AND REPROBATES

YOU WOULDN'T NORMALLY ASSOCIATE COLLECTING REPTILES WITH CRIME BUT, sadly, there's a thriving black-market trade in snakes, turtles and lizards, both for local collectors and to be sent overseas. This has been brought home to us directly over the years when we've had a few snakes and turtles stolen. In fact, it still goes on. I recently had problems with someone trying to net the last of my turtles. I didn't catch the thieves but they lost their net down in the pond, which is how I discovered the intrusion had occurred.

Quite a few years ago, two brothers came to the house. Their name was Nicol and they wanted to buy some little turtles from us. They went to George's place first and he brought them to me, but I said, 'I'm not selling turtles and no, I'm not breeding them.' They certainly dressed the part, with army fatigues on and really good high boots. I commented on this.

'Oh yeah,' one of them said. 'They're good for walking in the bush.'

Away they went, but I was a bit suspicious of them and so was George. We went back down to George's place, two doors away, and his wife, Moira, said: 'I don't know who those blokes were but they bought a couple of George's lizards.'

George and I went out with them while they put the lizards in their car and we saw cane cages in there. They had a few animals in them that they must have bought somewhere else.

'That's an unusual sort of a cage,' George said, but the bloke didn't comment.

A couple of weeks later, it was coming up to Christmas Eve when I discovered all my rare turtles had been knocked off from the hot room at the back of the house. There was no back fence at the time and there'd been a lot of rain, so there were clear footprints, including distinctive patterns from the same boots in two different sizes.

'That's them, the bastards,' I said.

Unbeknown to us, Moira had written their rego plate number down and, through a mate who'd sold specimens to a couple of blokes fitting their description, we tracked them down to where they lived in Bondi. We told the cops about them, and they were interested, apart from one smartarse mug detective.

'There's a man here says his turtle's been stolen,' he was singing out to all his mates. 'His little pet turtle's been stolen.'

These were specimens I had brought down from the Gulf Country and this ignorant copper was geeing me up. I thought, 'If we weren't in a police station, I'd show you "pet turtle", all right.'

The coppers weren't going to do anything right away, so George and I went to the address and knocked on the door. This bloke opened up and, sure enough, it was the two Nicol brothers. They argued with us but I could see they had a couple of our snakes, including some little pythons, there—but no turtles. We didn't realise at the time that the turtles were in a garage in units nearby in little ponds and tanks, but they weren't about to give them up.

'Well, we've been to the police and we know who you are and where you live,' I said. 'You tell me where the turtles are and we'll drop the charges.'

'Tell them f . . . n nothing,' the older brother said.

But the younger bloke said he'd tell us if we did agree to drop the charges. So I got all my turtles back. True to my word, I went back to the coppers with George and I told them we wanted to drop the charges.

'Okay, I'll drop the charges,' the detective said. 'But I've done a lot of paperwork about this and if you drop the charges, don't ever come back here in the future asking us for help with anything else.'

'Well, I never made any agreement,' George said. 'I'll charge them.'

So they were arrested and released on bail. One of them shot through; the other brother went to court, was found guilty and did six months in jail. It turned out they were notorious big-time animal smugglers and even made it into Raymond Hoser's book *Smuggled* about the illegal trade in reptiles, birds and other animals. It seems they were still doing it, even after one had been jailed and the other jumped bail. In fact, I'm told that John Nicol, the bail jumper, had travelled in and out of the country several times—so much for Border Security.

The Nicols were the most notorious animal traffickers we came across, but they weren't the worst criminals we encountered, not by a long shot. Back in the mid-1960s we were getting a few reptiles stolen and never had a clue who it was. Some good lizards went from George's yard so we asked around and some local youngsters said they knew where we could find the kids who'd knocked off our lizards. They said it was the Murphy boys who lived nearby, in Hastings Avenue, Chifley. So George and I went to their house. The boys were only young—one of them was about thirteen and the others about six and eight—and we said straight off that we knew they had our lizards and we wanted them back.

Well, you wouldn't believe the foul-mouthed abuse we got from these kids. They were cursing and swearing, screaming at us, like they were out of control. Then their grandmother came out and she was even worse than them with her obscene and aggressive curses and threats.

'I think we'll drop this, George,' I said. 'No lizard is worth all this.' So we told them we'd better not catch them near our place or there'd be trouble and we walked away.

'You know, those kids scared me,' I said to George when we got to the corner.

'Me too,' he said.

Twenty years later those kids became better known as the Murphy boys who abducted, raped and murdered Anita Cobby.

Our properties opened straight on to the bush so we were always a bit vulnerable to thieves and I eventually had to fit alarms to the snake and reptile houses. But I recall Pop telling me about a bunch of blokes running an illegal two-up game that had been raided by the cops and ran for it with the cops on their heels, running through backyards and gardens. One of them got to our place and saw a wall and thought it would be handy to hide behind. So over he goes and drops down into a snake pit with maybe 200 or so snakes in it. He screams like a banshee and takes off, hurdling the garden fences like an Olympic athlete. I doubt the police ever caught him.

One brush with lawlessness has nothing to do with snakes or turtles but still sends a shiver down my spine. Around Christmas 1977, I'd gone on a diving trip with my mate Trevor Allen. We used to call Trevor 'Saltwater Cecil' because he made his money out of selling sea water to aquariums. Trevor had a good business, especially when restaurants started installing lobster tanks.

Once he was called in by the Blue Angel restaurant in East Sydney, down from Kings Cross, which was a pretty notorious area back in the day. Their lobsters were dying and they couldn't keep them alive. Trevor supplied the water to them and he worked out what the trouble was right away. He rigged up refrigerators under the tanks and pumped chilled water into them to keep the temperature down. When the water was cold the lobsters survived for a long time.

Trevor was one of the first to supply salt water for aquariums. He lived at Botany and he used to get his water off Bare Island using plastic drums, pipes and pumps. He'd just park his wagon there and draw the water out where it was clearest. At least, he did until a National Parks bloke came along one day.

'What are you doing?' said the ranger.

'I'm getting salt water,' Trevor replied.

'You can't take salt water from here,' the ranger replied. 'This is a Marine National Park.'

I can't believe that. It's not like there's a water shortage in the ocean!

But I digress. I was down at Trevor's holiday place near Jervis Bay and he asked me if I wanted to go line fishing one night. I was never a keen line fisherman, but I'd done it and it was all right. Out we went through Murrays Beach, where there's a good ramp—and where in 1969 the idiot federal government proposed building a nuclear power station! Thank the lord they changed their mind, because Jervis Bay is one of the prettiest parts of Australia.

We put the boat in and headed out between Bowen Island and Governors Head, heading south. We went around two points but the wind was blowing pretty strongly and it wasn't comfortable, so we pulled into a little cove and stopped in close to the cliff. We dropped anchor and got the line in, sitting nice and quiet, hardly talking.

We were only there for a few minutes when we spotted a big freighter of some sort heading north. We were just sitting there watching it, and the next thing we saw some flashes of light from the ship, like from a signalling lamp. Flash, flash, flash—nothing more.

'Trevor, what the friggin hell is that?' I said.

'I don't know,' he replied.

Immediately a big bloody powerful motorboat kicked over just around the bend from where we were. It flew out, full bore, towards the ship.

'Let's friggin get out of here,' I said to Trevor, and he didn't need any persuasion.

We got back around to the boat ramp as fast as we could. There was at least one other car there, and a trailer, may be two cars—we didn't hang around to check. That's the last time we ever went fishing at night. That definitely had to be a drug pick-up. Remember, there were no mobile phones back then and by the time we'd got back to Trevor's and called the cops and they'd come from wherever they were based, there wasn't much point so we just let it go. The blokes in the powerboat would have been long gone.

But it all came back to me a few months later, on 23 September 1978, to be exact, when the Olympic swimmer Gary Chapman and his mate Ron Nelson disappeared on a fishing trip. They'd sailed out of Sylvania, heading for a fishing ground 15 kilometres off Maroubra. Their boat was found, capsized, the next day at Little Bay, with no sign of either of them.

Gary and I were friends. I'd come fourth to him in a swimming heat in the New South Wales School Championships. A couple of months later, Gary came third to me in the hurdles. We were good mates and hung out together at the Melbourne Olympics.

Gary had been a record-breaking distance swimmer as a kid but had dropped down to the sprints because Murray Rose was on the rise and Gary wanted to increase his chances of a medal. In fact, Gary got bronze when Australia completed a clean sweep in the 100-metres freestyle.

And that's what puzzled me. He was a champion swimmer and an experienced fisherman with a good boat, and he had a mate with him, but they were both gone. The boat drifted in but they never found the bodies.

Yes, I know there are freak waves and if one bloke gets into trouble he can take the bloke that's rescuing him down with him. But I can't help wondering if they were in the wrong place at the wrong time. And I often wonder what the blokes in the powerboat would have done if they'd spotted Trevor and me or we'd gone into their cove. They would surely have heard our motor and if it had been a drug drop, who knows what they'd have done?

It's all ifs and buts, but I'm putting that down as a bullet dodged, for us if not for Gary and his mate.

CHAPTER 24

NO FORTUNE, NO FAME

ALTHOUGH WE KEPT THE SNAKE SHOW GOING FOR FOUR DECADES AFTER POP passed away, George and I never made that much money from it. On a really good day, we could get $200 when we passed the hat around at the end of the show, but that was the exception rather than the rule, and it barely covered our expenses for catching and keeping the snakes. There was an interesting and fairly lucrative sideline, however, that led to us both ending up in Hollywood movies.

I can't remember exactly how it started, but there were a lot of kids' TV shows with nature segments in them—and youngsters are fascinated by snakes and lizards. Naturally enough, when they were looking for someone to demonstrate snakes, they came to us, just as they used to call Pop for that sort of thing. After a while it made sense for us to put a listing in *The Production Book*, a trade directory for anything and everything to do with

TV and film production. You want a lighting technician or a set designer or a make-up person—or a snake wrangler—you go to *The Production Book*.

We provided snakes for lots of TV dramas; snakes have been part of Australian storytelling as far back as Henry Lawson and Banjo Paterson, and they make for scary TV. So they'd call me or George up and ask if we could supply snakes and, of course, look after them on set. I used to supply brown snakes and tiger snakes for a lot of the different TV shows, and commercials as well. I had spiders and lizards too, and on any given day I could be driving around with a tiger snake and a couple of turtles in my car.

The movies were the best-paying gigs, though—money is no object for those fellas. One production in Queensland wanted to use a big sea turtle, but the Queensland wildlife people wouldn't let them because they were a protected species. So they called me and asked for the biggest turtle I had.

They flew me up to Queensland and flew me out to the island, but the weather was too bad for filming. So there I was, stuck in a motel with a bloody huge Mary River turtle. So I put some water in the bath and let the thing swim around in there, but I forgot about the room-service maid, and when she came in to clean the room she got a bit of a shock when she went in the bathroom.

I apologised profusely but she said it was okay and asked me what I fed it. I said bananas, and the next thing, the maids were in the bathroom, feeding bananas to my turtle. The weather got no better so they flew me back to Sydney, but before I could get back, an environmentalist group complained about me flying a turtle up to Queensland. Then the Queensland government got involved and they refused to give the movie producers permission to bring a turtle into the state. My turtle and I got a good trip up there the first time, anyway. And I was well paid and the turtle was well fed.

My biggest brush with fame came in 1988–89 when they were filming a telemovie called *Trouble in Paradise*, starring Raquel Welch and Jack Thompson. Raquel shot to fame in 1966 as the star of *1 Million Years B.C.*, and she was still in pretty good shape at close to 50 years old. The movie was about a posh American woman who is shipwrecked on a desert island with an uncouth Aussie yobbo, played by Jack Thompson.

At one point, Jack's character is supposed to have this big, hairy spider crawling all over him, so they paid me to get a big bird-eating spider. I got one from my mate Peter in Queensland. The bird-eating spider rarely eats birds, but it's big enough to, and its fangs are huge and, although its venom isn't the deadliest, it can give you a nasty bite.

'Are they cranky?' I asked Pete.

'Oh, they can be,' he said. 'If you want to handle them you've got to use a big wooden spoon and pick them up that way.'

So I put the spider down on my back lawn and tapped him with the big wooden spoon. Was he cranky? He reared up like a funnel web, waving his front legs and showing his fangs and I thought, 'Jeez, this is going to be interesting.' When I picked him up on the stick, though, he was all right. Down we went to Darling Harbour, where they were shooting the dockside scenes, and the stuntman who was going to be Jack's stand-in, came up and said, 'Give us a look at this spider, John.'

I tipped the spider out and the stuntman was clearly taken aback at the size of it.

'Does he bite?' he says.

'Oh, I don't think so,' I replied. 'Just handle him gently and you'll be fine.'

I gave the spider a gentle tap and he reared up again, like before, all fangs and furry legs.

'No f . . . n' way!' said the stuntman. 'No way am I going anywhere near that!'

He walked over and told the assistant director he wasn't touching the spider. End of story. Then the AD came over to me and asked what we could do. I shrugged—I'd done my bit. I wasn't there to wrangle the stuntman.

'Would you do it?' he asked.

'Yeah,' I said. 'If you pay me enough.'

And so I was paid both for providing the spider and for standing in for the suddenly spider-wary stuntman. Best of all, it was Saturday and I was supposed to be working at ICI on double time but my mates covered for me, so I got double time for my day job and double time for the spider.

All I had to do was lie face-up with my shirt off. They darkened me up a little bit with make-up. Even though I was pretty brown, I wasn't as dark as Jack because he was supposed to be in the sun all day. Then they put his medallion chain on me and that's what you see in the movie as the spider crawls around and up my neck and around my ears.

If you've ever been on a TV or movie set, you'll know that they keep doing the scenes over and over again, and there must have been about ten takes of this spider crawling all over me. I'd had enough already when the spider decided to wander off.

'No, bring him back again, John,' one of the crew says.

'*You* friggin bring him back,' I said. As if I was going to go and pick him up and put him on my neck. But it was all right and I got good money and it went over pretty well.

As for meeting Raquel, I remember they had a bar room set with fake cigarette smoke pumped into it and lots of Chinese actors and extras to make it look like it was in Hong Kong. I was sitting out on the verandah with a couple of the Asian extras who'd come out for a breath of fresh air, and the next thing out came this gorgeous woman. She stretches out her arms and breathes in deeply, showing off her assets.

'Oh, I detest that smoke,' she says to me. 'It's killing me.'

So here's my chance to say something clever and witty, maybe even a bit flirtatious, to one of the most beautiful women in the world.

'Yeah,' I say, 'it's not real pleasant, is it?'

Not real pleasant?! Chance of a lifetime and I was tongue-tied.

George went one better than me the following year, not in talking to a Hollywood heartthrob but in appearing in a proper made-for-cinema movie. The film was *Quigley Down Under*, with Tom Selleck (then famous as Magnum PI) in the title role and the late Alan Rickman as the baddie. I don't know exactly what George's role was, but I doubt he was as easily flummoxed by the stars as I was by the lovely Ms Welch.

CHAPTER 25

SURVIVOR

BY THE TIME YOU READ THIS BOOK, I WILL HAVE CELEBRATED MY 80TH BIRTHDAY (I hope) surrounded by my family, camped on the upper reaches of the Macleay River. If writing this book has taught me anything, it's that I've had a pretty eventful life. I've competed in one Olympic games, where I made lifelong friends, and was part of the torch relay for the Sydney Games in 2000. I've acquired a shoebox full of athletics medals, played rugby league for New South Wales with some legends of the game, and fought deadset champions in the boxing ring.

I've survived rickets, snakebites, a broken neck, a stroke, cancer and being shot at by Indonesian soldiers in New Guinea. I've been ripped off by kids who went on to be killers, cheated by bungling bureaucrats and robbed by corrupt officials . . . and a charming young woman on a German train.

I've written nine books and a stack of scientific papers, and identified many new species of Australian turtle, occasionally making waves. I've been invited to give the keynote speech at conferences in the United States, where hundreds of my peers turned up to hear me, and I've given a talk to an empty room in New Zealand.

Somewhere along the way, I acquired a brilliant family: my loving wife Helen, three great kids and eight grandkids (not one of whom has the slightest interest in snakes!).

In 1992, I was awarded the Order of Australia for 'service to conservation and the environment, particularly through natural history, and to the community'. It was Keith Smith, who compiled the two volumes of *Johnny Cann: Nature Boy*, who got the ball rolling. The first I heard of it was when I got a letter asking me if I'd accept the honour if it was offered to me (they don't want to offer it to someone who might throw it back at them).

So on a beautiful autumn day on 1 May 1992, Helen, Paul and I went to Government House in Sydney, where I was invested in the Order of Australia by the New South Wales Governor, Rear Admiral Peter Sinclair. It was a proud moment that many would take as the culmination of their career—but I still had a few years left in me.

I carried on doing the snake shows, alternating with George until he became too ill to continue and then passed away. My last public show at the Loop was in April 2010. The federal MP

Peter Garrett and state MP Michael Daley were both there and presented me with a plaque and certificates. There was a big mob there that day, with TV cameras (one of my friends from down south who was too sick to attend paid for a professional film crew to record the event for him), the lot, and I only did three shows. I was pretty slow but it was quite good.

We had a big party after. It wasn't organised but it just spontaneously occurred in my backyard where there wasn't even standing room. A lot of my mates came from interstate for the last show, including one who came down from Darwin. We had a pretty good night.

I think I might have got out of the snake game just in time. Two years later I suffered a pretty serious stroke, and when the doctors did a scan to see what damage had been done, they reckoned they'd found cancer in my kidney and my brain. I don't remember much about that conversation—I wasn't thinking too clearly—but all my family was standing around nice and quiet, and whispering to each other and to the doctors, as well as to me.

Eventually, Paul, my elder son said, 'Well what's the bottom line, Doc? Give us the results.'

'With the cancer in his brain and his kidneys, I consider that your father has got about two and a half weeks to live,' he said.

My youngest bloke Jace is a really quiet kid, but Paul and Helen had to grab him and pull him away because he was about to have a pop at the doctor for being so blunt in front of his mum. Later on I discovered that Paul had asked the doctor if the two scans showing the cancer were the same colour. The doctor looked surprised and said, 'No, no they're not.'

'Well that doesn't mean they're both cancer, does it?' Paul said.

'You could be right, Paul,' the doctor said.

Afterwards they decided it wasn't cancer in my brain after all, and after six months of investigation the surgeon decided it was actually the bleed that had caused the stroke. That said, the Prince of Wales Hospital staff, the specialists and the doctors were pretty good. I was in hospital for a few weeks and then when I was strong enough they removed the diseased kidney, and then everything sort of came good.

I still wonder whether it was a cancer or a dead kidney, to tell the truth, because tiger snake venom can kill kidneys— the Commonwealth Serum Laboratories have done papers on it. I did mention that to the doctors. A very good snakey mate of mine called Vic Hayden had a stroke, same as me, and we were on the same tablets, but five months later Vic was stone dead with complete kidney failure. It was the tiger snake that killed Vic.

A couple of days after I had the stroke I was supposed to be going to the Galápagos Islands. A mate of mine is a professor at Chapman University, in the city of Orange, California, and they had raised funds so that a number of us could fly out and go on a big cruise boat with a group of students. Helen didn't want to go so Jace was coming with me. That was naturally called off when I had the stroke, but twelve months later they said, 'Well, you can come this year.'

So in January 2013, Jace and I went there and I celebrated my 75th birthday aboard the cruise boat, the *Tip Top II*. We were out diving nearly every day on that trip. At one point I went down 5 metres and Jace took a picture of me with his underwater camera. I just put my thumb up in the air and rolled over on the coral. I got a mate to email the picture to the doctor who'd said I had two weeks to live. I didn't put my name on it—just my patient number at the hospital, which I know off by heart, I've been there that many times. I know he received it and that if he was curious, he would have looked it up, but he never replied.

So, as I approach my 80th birthday, I'm doing all right for an old bloke. My new book on turtles came out last year and I've been having operations on my eyes, which have delayed another trip to America, but that will be back on soon.

The venomous snakes have gone from my pits. You have to be on your toes and have your wits about you, especially when your next snakebite could be your last. But my old mate the water dragon is still out the back, nodding his head as he soaks up the sun.

A couple of people from the herpetological society have taken over the snake shows at the Loop, but for the first time in 100 years, there's no one there with the name of Cann tempting fate and wondering if the next tiger or brown will be the one that gets him.

So you can still catch a snake show on a Sunday in the pit at La Pa. But I am the last of the snake-handling Canns, happy to make way for the next generation of snakeys to inspire and amaze the kids who will continue this great tradition.

AUSTRALIA'S GREAT SNAKEYS

THE GREAT 'PROFESSOR FOX', WHO STARTED THE SNAKE SHOWS AT LA PEROUSE, no doubt inspired my father to follow in his footsteps, and my mother also recalled a long procession of snake men and women who came and went—some permanently after their snakes got the better of them or they decided that their first serious bite was one too many. Some were truly great performers with either a magic potion that worked (unlikely) or a level of acquired resistance that protected them from snakebites. Others discovered the hard way that whatever protection they thought they had was illusory. And some were charlatans, only working with snakes or reptiles that had been defanged and milked—although even that was no guarantee of safety. You can't milk a deadly snake dry—they will always have some venom there as they are constantly producing it. Whatever the reality of their acts, the snake shows were incredibly popular in the sideshow alleys of travelling funfairs and country agricultural shows.

In 1978, I realised that the memories of the old snake shows were dying out as rapidly as the trade's less well-protected operators so I wrote a book that documented for the first time this arcane corner of show business before it disappeared forever. The book, *Snakes Alive*, published by Kangaroo Press, won a number of awards and commendations. An updated version was published in 1986 by Eco Press in the USA. The stories that follow are drawn from its pages.

For a while in Australia the market for snake acts was strong enough to even attract foreign performers like the half-French Princess Indita and the American Latiefa 'Queen of Reptiles', both known for working with rattlesnakes. The shows were not uniformly welcomed by government bodies, however, and the snakeys were increasingly banned. This meant the snake men and women had to find other specialties to entertain the crowds.

Vince Labb took his snakes to Shepparton in 1912, for example, but was prevented from exhibiting them. So he became instead the 'Handcuff King', and photos show him at the Shepparton showground in front of a tent proclaiming 'The Escapist', with chains hanging from his shoulders and arms like great iron pythons.

And while the travelling shows encountered a wide range of by-laws and restrictions, some more permanent venues were also evolving. Not many people owned their own vehicles, and public transport was in great demand. At many a tram terminus—such as Manly, Coogee, La Perouse, Botany, Bondi and Brighton—fairgrounds sprang up, prospered and remained for many years.

Needless to say, snake shows became regular and popular attractions, feeding off the fear and dread of the spectators while claiming their share of the lives of usually fledgling performers and a few 'snake-oil salesmen'. These last were really no more than antidote vendors who, after seeing seasoned showmen take a snakebite and then treat it, felt there was an easy quid in putting on a show. Some of them thought the trick was to defang and milk the snakes, then make it look like the antidote was effective. They would discover to their cost that this was not the case and deaths haunted the acts, although many of them went unrecorded or received only scant media attention.

'He was unable to talk, but wrote down that he was twice bitten when handling a tiger snake some six hours earlier,' states the obituary for one unnamed victim. 'Walsford Fowler considered himself immune and used to walk around with a green tree snake around his neck . . . caught adder . . . brought to hotel . . . died the next day,' reads another. Many such victims would have been snake pit men who never got off the ground . . . just ended up under it.

Snake handling changed through the first half of the twentieth century, for a number of reasons: the increasing availability

THE LAST SNAKE MAN

of antivenom made it a lot less hazardous, the snakeys themselves tended to avoid being bitten if they could (rather than trading on their ability to survive bites), and the growing attractions of TV made the old sideshows largely redundant.

Meanwhile, however, as long as there were audiences around, there were dozens of snakeys plying their trade. The denizens of the La Perouse Loop you've met already. Here are some of the other great snake men and women of Australia.

'Professor' Jim Morrissey

There was possibly no snake man better at drawing the crowds and holding them than the self-styled 'Professor' Jim Morrissey, also known as 'Morrissey of the Snakes'.

Born in London in 1849, he was the son of a stonemason and emigrated to Tasmania when he was twenty. Two decades later he got his introduction to Australian snakes by obtaining contracts to rid them from country properties by killing them. He subsequently claimed that because he knew so much about snakes he was entitled to call himself 'Professor'.

He was a great talker and his trademark was a battered felt hat with a ligature, or tourniquet, for a band. He was popular with journalists seeking a few paragraphs, and in 1909 became probably the first snake handler to be employed by an education department to lecture on reptiles in schools.

Eventually the professor set up shop in Bourke Street, Melbourne, though through inclination or necessity he supplemented his income by some less than legal activities. These, coupled with a taste for the bottle, resulted in run-ins with the law—not that he was unwilling to turn even these misfortunes to his quick-thinking advantage. But snakes were Morrissey's living and he was certainly versatile.

'There's lots of ways of turning money from snakes,' he said. 'First, there's the antidote which, with the ligature I've got a provisional patent on, I've sold to thousands of people from Tasmania to Queensland. Then there's the venom, and I've sold some of that to the university. Then there's the skin, to be made up into belts an' bags an' slippers; and the belts themselves—I've often got 35 shillings for a good belt by rafflin' it in a billiard room,' he boasted.

Morrissey claimed that exhibitions and collections at racecourses, and private demonstrations in a cosy little room, or 'public yappin' to a crowd in front of a hotel' all produced cash. In fact, Morrissey said that at times he had made as much as 100 pounds a week, including a 'cheque for £50 sent to the missis' by a man whose boy's life he had saved.

Summing up life as a snake-man entrepreneur, he once said, 'I've had money for catchin' snakes, and even for lettin' snakes kill me—if they could. I've earned a pound apiece gettin' snakes out of wells and cellars, and I've been paid half-a-crown a head by McKenna's brewery for catchin' 'em in the barley crop when the men threatened to knock off work, they was so bad.'

One of his most colourful encounters was witnessed by a well-known journalist, W.A. Somerset, and recounted in Melbourne's *Life* magazine. In 1915, Princess Indita arrived in Australia from the United States. Her forte was the 'weird snake dance of the Hopi Indians', which she performed in vaudeville shows. Morrissey learnt she was to give a private exhibition for the press and certain favoured citizens, performing with rattlesnakes, which Morrissey had not encountered before, so he went along. She told him her favourite snakebite antidote was an American Indian one that had been handed to her by her father's tribe, but often she just used iodine or salt.

Morrissey was not impressed and, pulling out a phial of his own brownish cure-all, said, 'I'll back this little old bottle against this Yankee tail-shaker. He may have a row like a bloomin' spinning jenny, but for quickness, dash and for venom, give me the Australian tiger anytime.'

'What's more,' he challenged, 'I'll come here any night you like an' prove it before an audience.' Princess Indita agreed and a few nights later at the Bijou Theatre, after she'd performed for a spellbound audience, a short, elderly man in a grey suit and battered felt hat strolled onto the boards, and the audience rose as one and cheered.

Morrissey stirred the rattlesnake with his toe and it struck but landed between his feet, which were wide apart. He stuck his arm towards the snake and this time the rattler made no mistake, biting him just above his wrist. He whacked it on the nose with his free hand so the reptile reverted to its coiled stance.

The bite looked bad and was bleeding freely. Tom 'Pambo' Eades, a snake-man friend, was in the audience and immediately went up on stage to help to apply the antidote and scarify the wound, cutting a line in the skin from one puncture hole to the other, a standard preparation for the application of antidote.

Morrissey was unconcerned, but the Princess stood spell-bound by this rash display of foolhardiness from the 66-year-old showman. All was not quite as well as Morrissey made out, however. Later that night he collapsed and was taken to Melbourne Hospital. When he awoke he found himself in strange surroundings and yelled, 'What am I here for?' On being told he said, 'That's all right. Just bring me my clothes. Oh, and thanks for the help.' And within minutes he was up, dressed and had discharged himself.

Morrissey was constantly on the move and showed little sign of his age as the years advanced. He seemed always to be seeking a crowd, though after a few drinks he could be equally adept at breaking up the people or the furniture. Morrissey had patented his antidote in 1912, and a pamphlet supplied with the bottle quoted a story from the *Northern Star*: 'A lad named Arthur Vagne while snake hunting at Gundurimba was bitten by a snake. The reptile was of the black species, with bright red underneath. Vagne had a bottle of Morrissey's Antidote with him. He at once applied the ligature, scarified the bitten part and applied the antidote. Afterwards, no ill effects of the bite were experienced.'

Given the unusual name it seems likely that the lad was a relative of Rocky Vagne (later Vane) who by that time was becoming as famous as Morrissey—in fact, the two teamed up for a spell or two. Things became tougher for Morrissey in his declining years, however, and it's said that he had to 'hump the bluey' (become a swagman) on the open roads of the Hawkesbury district. He died at Parramatta in an aged-care home on 7 August 1929 at the age of 80—not a bad innings for a 'feller that was easily satisfied and doesn't want to live forever'.

Tom Wanless

Tom Wanless was not the first showman to trade off the name of a predecessor, but in calling himself 'Young Morrissey', he linked his career to Australia's most flamboyant snake man. Wanless claimed that he had every justification in taking Jim Morrissey's name.

Research reveals few details of Wanless's early life. It's said he was born in Victoria in 1895 and orphaned at six, to which he added the claim that he was then cared for by the self-confessed reprobate Jim Morrissey, who 'induced me to study snakes and in that work we were inseparable. If he got a bite, I got a bite.'

Whether this is true or not, Wanless made the claim while Morrissey was still alive—and in fact, the older man outlived him by eight years.

In an effort to disassociate himself from Wanless, Morrissey contacted *Truth* newspaper, which gleefully publicised his indignant plea to 'have placed on record through the columns of the only paper worth reading that the individual Thomas Wanless, who is alleged to bear also the "MORRISSEY" moniker is no relative and incidentally no friend of the "Professor". The little weather-beaten and mentally acute old 'un wishes it known, that he did not, as has been stated, adopt Wanless, the "younger Morrissey" for the very good and sufficient reason that it has at times taken the old fellow all his time to adopt himself.'

Morrissey was a garrulous self-promoter at the best of times, but the tone of his renunciation of Wanless's claims smacks of more than a mere family rift. The earliest objective report of Tom Wanless's career dates from 1913, when the teenage 'confectioner' of Lawson Street, Balmain, was bitten on the chin by a red-bellied black snake more than 2 metres long. He was rushed to Sydney Hospital in a serious condition, but lived to charm again.

A few years later, Wanless extended his snake-show venues to take in the La Perouse Loop, along with the Hessells (see Chapter 1), and in March 1920, there being no import restrictions on reptiles, Wanless, as 'Young Morrissey', showed an American copperhead snake in Balmain and was bitten.

'Like a flash, the fangs of the cold-blooded immigrant were buried into his upper lip,' a journalist recorded, 'and in a couple of seconds, Morrissey was taking the count. But in just half a minute he was around again, having given the antidote one of the greatest tests it had ever been put to.'

Later, Morrissey said: 'A great sickness came over me. I felt as if I was choking, as if my glands had grown monstrously. It seemed as if all my teeth were failing out and then I seemed to be paralysed. I take seven or eight bites a week, mostly at private exhibitions, the bite of a tiger snake being most severe. It will be a tiger bite that will settle me in the long run. The punishment is too great on the heart, but I never think of that. Time enough to worry about death when we come to it, whether it delivers the knock by snake poison or by dieting yourself carefully so that senile decay sets in.'

Later in 1920, Wanless teamed up with Dave Meekin, one of Australia's best middleweight boxers. They made a rough-and-ready knockabout pair, with Wanless as fond of the bottle as he was of snakes and Meekin addicted to fisticuffs and the fairground. Meekin was contracted to fight for the South African big-game hunter John Burger, and Wanless—now calling himself Morrissey—went along to South Africa for the ride. Burger and Wanless soon became firm friends.

According to Burger, Wanless stood only 5 feet tall and weighed barely 50 kilograms. He had three top front teeth missing and wore a red scarf around his neck, the ends pulled through a gold ring studded with two diamonds. He invariably dressed in an open khaki shirt, a pair of riding breeches and top boots.

Early in their friendship, Wanless bullied Burger into taking him by rickshaw to a snake-infested plantation. Within a couple of hours Wanless had caught a 2-metre green mamba, known to the Africans as the 'cloud of death' and one of the world's deadliest snakes. To Burger's astonishment, Wanless managed to get the snake into his shirt. 'His belt and button were securely fastened and, for additional security, my tie was fastened around his neck below the collar,' he wrote.

When they returned to town Wanless advertised that he would accept a bite from the mamba that night at 9 p.m. When the time arrived, the showman's tent was packed to suffocation. After teasing the mamba, Wanless grabbed it by the head and pushed his forearm under the snake's snout. When the fangs sank into his arm, Wanless released his grip and let the reptile hang from his arm for some seconds, supported only by its fangs.

The mamba was then removed and placed in a cage, after which Wanless showed his bleeding arm to the crowd. Incisions were made and Wanless's antidote was poured into the wound. On completion of the treatment, Wanless told the watchers that the following night he would allow himself to be bitten by a puff adder. The crowd was reluctant to leave and those who hung on for purely ghoulish reasons were not disappointed. Wanless collapsed within a few minutes and showed signs of neurotoxic poisoning: his breathing was affected, his pupils dilated and his pulse raced.

But the following day he was up and about, though much less sprightly than usual, which meant he had to postpone further displays of recklessness by 24 hours. Over the next week, however, Burger claimed to have seen Wanless accept bites from a black mamba, cobras and puff adders. On one occasion, three doctors examined a mamba before it bit him and declared it to be venomous. At another display, a sceptical audience taunted Wanless into also allowing a dog to be bitten: the dog died and Wanless was fined 10 pounds.

Always a heavy drinker, Wanless began to overindulge and was soon in constant conflict with Meekin. But there was never a physical fight, since the smaller man compensated for his size by carrying a snake in his shirt, declaring that if Meekin ever tried to hit him, he would 'give him the snake treatment'.

One night, while visibly affected by drink, Wanless handled a puff adder roughly and it bit into his thumbnail. The fang broke off and a doctor was called in the next day when the thumb was clearly poisoned. Once more, however, Wanless cheated death, but as with most daredevil showmen, it was only a matter of time before he received a fatal bite. Tom Wanless's turn came on 18 July 1921 and two letters received by the Sydney *Sunday Times* tell the story.

The first was signed 'Alby Jackson, Showman, late of Glebe, Sydney': 'Knowing the favours the late Tom Morrissey [*sic*] owed to your journal and being an intimate fellow Australian Pal of his, I am penning a note Re his death, which occurred here on the 18th of July, after taking his 10th snakebite.

'The last snake he chose was the deadly South African "Green Mamba," said by experts to be even deadlier than the Indian "Krait", that killed Professor Fox. Young Tom Morrissey, perhaps the gamest Aussie I have met, allowed himself to be bitten on the arm at 8 o'clock on Saturday night. By 4 o'clock the following morning, Tom developed bad symptoms, wreathing [sic] blood. At 10 o'clock he had a look at himself in the mirror and calmly remarked "The Green Mamba wins". He lingered on till the next day, and died a martyr to his business, Snake Bite.

'All Australians in Durban followed "Young Tom" to his last resting place, as he was a great favourite here, his gameness attracting attention.'

The second letter was from Meekin, who alluded to the rift with Wanless and to a lack of responsible management: 'I am sorry to say poor Tom was not showing under my Banners at the time,' wrote Meekin, who also mentioned the previous bite to the thumb, and that Wanless's general health was not great and he was in no condition to take a bite from such a dangerous snake as a mamba.

'I . . . begged of him to leave it out for a while and give himself a fighting chance to recover thoroughly,' wrote Meekin. 'However, he would not be advised. We are to bury him tomorrow at 11.30 o'clock.'

A fairly lurid piece from the South African press titled 'The Man Who Shook Hands With Death' by H. Lloyd Watkins noted Tom Wanless's fatalism: 'Many times I have stood and watched and listened to young Tom's quiet and natural lectures on his "friends", as he was always pleased to call them, when he has been surrounded by sceptics.

'"If I fasten this reptile on my body," he would say, "and you saw me go from red to black and fall foaming, to die before your eyes, you would go out and say, 'By God! it was no fake; the snakes were poisonous, right enough. How awful.' But just because I save myself and smile a few minutes afterwards, you all likewise smile, and mutter, 'Fraud!' 'Impostor!' Someday— who knows?—you will see Tommy Morrissey go out. Then you'll believe; not before. I suppose I can't blame you—it's the way of the world!"

'He would then smile and take up another hissing reptile, and make friends with it before your eyes. Well, poor Tom, he said he would find death in the tent. He little guessed how soon.'

Rocky Vane

The son of a bootmaker and one of seven children, Lindsay Herbert Vagne was born on 19 July 1891 at Kangaroo Valley. The family soon moved north to Lismore, where it is still represented, and young Lindsay was apprenticed to Kleins, a firm of coach builders. A knockabout young man who earned his nickname

'Rocky', Vagne was also a snake collector from an early age, and a chance meeting with Jim Morrissey led to him embracing showmanship as avidly as he had snakes. Soon Vagne had built a large iron shed on the outskirts of Lismore, installed a snake pit, and hung out a banner quaintly reading 'Snaix'. Deep-voiced and prematurely grey, he cut a dash as a showman, and developed into an excellent spruiker.

Soon Rocky had dropped the 'g' from his French grandfather's name, assembled his own travelling snake show, and hit the road as Rocky Vane. In 1914 his partner Alex 'Sandy' Rolfe was bitten and killed by a tiger snake, but Vane was undeterred and kept his show on the move, sometimes in partnership with his early mentor, Jim Morrissey. In fact, Vane was one of the privileged few to be given the older man's formula for his snake-bite antidote.

Vane then developed his own variant, which probably varied even more from time to time, depending on his location and the materials available. It's most likely that the antidotes of both men were based on bracken ferns, beaten to a pulp and then boiled and strained. Salt and Condy's crystals (potassium permanganate) would then be added, with perhaps some boot polish for colour and 'finish'.

Years later, in 1934, the Vane and Morrissey antidotes and two others were tested by Dr Kellaway of Melbourne's Walter and Eliza Hall Institute, and it was noted that 'no protective action by any of these antidotes could be demonstrated'.

Back in the 1920s, however, Vane's fame was so widespread that a newspaper sent him to Bungowannah Station near Albury, to investigate the mysterious case of a worker there who had suffered an alarming number of snakebites. Vane soon got to the root of the problem when he discovered that the young jackaroo hadn't taken to station life and had faked bites, using a pin, to secure regular breaks in hospital.

In the early 1920s Rocky married Dorothy Whitley from Bangalow. Dot's family had show horses, which Rocky also adopted, along with a sharpshooting act. Vane then diversified even further by painting banners for fellow showmen and, while resting from constant touring, opened tattoo parlours at different times in Adelaide, Perth, Sydney and Melbourne.

Photographs of Rocky Vane at La Perouse show that he would allow himself to be bitten quite deliberately and then treat himself with his antidote. Sometimes after being bitten he would encourage the snake to bite a chicken to prove how deadly it was, though this was soon outlawed by the police.

Pop and Rocky remained in close contact, and would often team up for a show, both then capitalising on Vane's basso profundo voice and great skills as a spruiker. By the time Mum and Dad settled permanently in Sydney in 1926, the Vanes were working their way to Western Australia. Dot Vane had confessed to Mum that she was terrified of snakes—but she was still handling them, and by the time she'd reached Perth she was appearing as another in the long line of showground

'Cleopatras'. No female snake handlers had been seen in the west, and Rocky was expecting huge crowds . . . and got them, too, until January 1928 when he telegrammed Pop: 'Dot died this morning.'

At the inquest, Vane said that when a tiger snake bit his wife he had immediately applied a ligature and his antidote and sent her to hospital. The ligature was removed after three-quarters of an hour, after which Dot had discharged herself and returned to the showground. But she had a relapse and Rocky returned her to the hospital, where she died the next day. Rocky argued with the doctors that they had removed the ligature before the antidote had taken full effect, and that on his return he was not allowed to apply more antidote.

It was also revealed at the inquest that when Dot Vane returned to hospital, a second bite was discovered on the back of her thumb. It may have been overlooked when she was first admitted, but was more likely a fresh bite.

After Dot's death, Rocky took on another assistant, William Harry Melrose, a former partner of Pop's. One Sunday in February 1929, Melrose went to the Buffalo Club in Wellington Street, Perth, with a bag he told members contained performing frogs. Then, with an interested crowd around him, the trickster took out first a carpet snake and then a tiger snake, which petrified the onlookers and immediately bit Melrose. He was rushed to hospital where he died the following Wednesday.

Snake exhibitions were banned in the state as a result, but three days after Melrose's death, and aware that this edict was about to come into effect, Rocky allowed himself to be bitten on the thumb to demonstrate the power of his antidote. The performance was not altogether effective. Rocky collapsed and was taken to hospital, where he did recover, but not before he'd learnt the dangers of clashing with doctors. The ligature was left on for an agonisingly long time, and this resulted in loss of muscle tone so great that it took several months of exercise before Rocky regained full control of his limb.

Eight years later, doing a show at Redhill, South Australia, Rocky was bitten by a tiger snake and collapsed soon after. He was taken to Snowtown Hospital and later flown to Adelaide Hospital, where he was admitted in a critical condition. Rocky survived but slowed down as a snake handler after that, though his involvement with the pits didn't end completely. Pop remembered one occasion during a show when Rocky seemed to get increasingly intoxicated as the day progressed and the show boss grew equally frustrated because he couldn't find the source of his supply. Only when the show was over and the pit and tent dismantled did he find a pile of small bottles labelled 'Rocky Vane's Snakebite Cure' and smelling strongly of rum.

Rocky remarried, and his second wife, Joyce, also a show-woman, was soon handling snakes for the first time, and so successfully she never needed to rely on either antidote or anti-venom. During World War II the Vanes' business prospered.

They continued running snake shows around the Melbourne area, and Rocky's tattoo shop did a roaring trade with Allied servicemen.

In 1946 Rocky Vane became ill while arranging for permits to show snakes at the Hobart Regatta, and half an hour after the boat had sailed for Tasmania he suffered a stroke. He was returned to Melbourne and admitted to Latrobe Hospital, but died on 19 February, aged 55—a not inconsiderable age for a snake man.

Joyce Vane carried on performing with snakes after Rocky died and eventually taught her new husband, Tom Kerswell, the tricks of the snakey trade, although they eventually moved into a less hazardous form of sideshow, with roundabouts and knock-'em-downs.

Professor Victor Hullar

Another self-styled 'professor', Victor Hullar was an experienced snake man who advocated using leeches to extract venom from snakebites and had survived several himself. But during a performance in May 1893 his luck ran out. He had placed the head of a metre-long tiger snake into his mouth and was gripping it with his teeth while he held a 1.5-metre tiger snake in one hand and stroked it with the other.

Suddenly the snake being stroked darted its head out and sank its fangs into one of the professor's fingers. He calmly

THE LAST SNAKE MAN

returned both snakes to their box, took a nip of brandy and then rubbed some of his homemade antidote into the wound. Not long afterwards, Hullar began to tremble all over. A doctor gave him an injection of strychnine, then a controversial but popular snakebite treatment, but to no avail, and Hullar died the following day.

Harry Deline

Another ill-fated performer was the well-liked and highly respected Harry Deline. In December 1913 he set up at Melbourne's Luna Park, assisted by a young woman billed as 'Sleeping Beauty'. It was her job to lie full length on a stretcher and feign sleep while Deline placed venomous snakes all over her body.

On the night of his last performance, Deline had about 50 snakes in his temporary pit and was playing to a crowd of about as many people, mainly women and children. As he began placing the reptiles on his partner's inert body, a large tiger snake took offence and adopted a defence stance. Showing off, Deline picked up the snake at the middle of its body (a real error!) and held it aloft. The tiger struck at Harry's neck, biting him firmly about 12 millimetres from the jugular.

With blood running from the puncture marks, Deline pulled the snake away and returned it and its partners to their cage. Sleeping Beauty remained oblivious to the drama unfolding so near, and the crowd at first thought everything was part of the act. But when Deline turned deadly pale, staggered, and fell into the arms of an attendant, there was pandemonium. Thinking that the snakes would escape, women began to scream and many fainted.

A doctor was summoned from nearby St Kilda and he ordered the showman to be driven to Alfred Hospital. As it was dark, one of the headlights was taken from the vehicle and placed on the back seat so the doctor could attend to the victim in transit. The neck was carefully scarified, a difficult and dangerous job in itself as the car jolted on its way. Owing to the speed with which Deline received attention and the fact that he'd survived many bites in the past, it was expected he would recover. But he fell into a coma and died two and a half days later.

Sintau

Sintau, a glamorous snake man, was working with a German American called Brooks, who claimed to be afraid of no snake's bite. The reptiles were being freely handled by both men in front of a large crowd at Melbourne's Brighton Beach when Sintau announced that he was going to place a large brown snake's head in his mouth.

He took the reptile by its middle, whereupon the snake struck viciously at the bridge of his nose. The wound was bleeding freely as Brooks took the snake away and then attended to his partner's bite with some antidote or another. A short time later,

Sintau, who had presumably built up immunity, showed no ill effects. We can assume the sales of his antidote went through the roof that night—although it's unlikely it had any effect.

Captain Greenhalgh

When Professor Fox was fatally bitten by a krait in India, the *Sydney Mail* ran an almost-full-page obituary on 14 March 1914. But down in the bottom right-hand corner of the page there is also a report on the appearance of a new snake man, one Captain Greenhalgh, who was billed to perform at White City in Rushcutters Bay.

Later Sydney's tennis headquarters, early last century White City was one of Australia's show meccas, and up to 30,000 people a night would flock there to take a ride on the 'Mammoth Carousel' or take a gondola trip through cave scenery around an 'underground' river. Large bagging walls painted with white clouds gave the venue its name. And, of course, there were always snake shows.

Snake men by the name of Pambara, Long Tim Finlay and William Keeping, as well as Morrissey, Fred Fox, my father George Cann and many others, plied their trade there and vied for customers. Captain Greenhalgh—'handling deadly tiger snakes, just six inches in length, the first ever bred in captivity'—was a showman first and foremost, and no more than a dabbler in snakes. A year earlier he had appeared with the

American Latiefa, but in 1914 he was making something of a comeback, probably cashing in on the publicity surrounding the recent deaths of better-known snake men.

The Greenhalgh family was actually best known for its sharp-shooting shows. The captain, his son Arthur and daughter Miss Eddy had a popular act in the 1920s. Arthur also took on an American partner, Abe Jackson, a motorbike stunt rider formerly of the 'Reckless Jacksons'. The partnership prospered and diversified, taking in snake shows. Arthur was never a handler himself, but he employed many acts and in 1924 married the beautiful snake girl Navada, who, along with 'Cleopatra' Essie Bradley (later my mum), had worked the 1923 Sydney Royal Easter Show for him. Mrs Greenhalgh became widely known as 'Red', and worked the pits for several more years.

Fred and Belle Wade

The Greenhalghs also worked with the husband and wife team Fred and Belle Wade. Born in Victoria in 1898, Fred Wade knocked about with the snake man Marco Miller (see below) for many years and got into the snake game himself in the late 1920s.

Belle Wade had migrated from England in 1921, and it took her many years to overcome her fear of snakes. By 1930, however, she was handling venomous reptiles and participating fully in Fred's acts. Her show names included 'Monica Sans' and

'Venitia', and when the Wades teamed up with Greenhalgh and Jackson, the banners outside her show pit proclaimed her 'La Belle'.

The Wades were a famous couple, enjoying popularity with the crowds and the other show people alike. Not that the opposition was strong in the 1930s; the Millers were the only performers who could readily challenge the Wades' style and range of venomous and non-venomous snakes.

Crowds love large pythons, and the Wades accommodated them, making numerous collecting trips to North Queensland. While on these trips they made the Millaa Millaa Hotel, west of Innisfail, their base camp, and the publican allowed Fred to store his charges loose in a spare room. They said there was nothing to beat the sight of 6-metre pythons lying on the windowsills seeking the sun while daredevil drunks gathered outside, tapping on the glass.

A news clipping from 1928 reports that at Moira Lakes (just off the Murray River, north of Moama in New South Wales), Fred Wade was bitten by a 1.5-metre tiger snake and managed to drive only part of the way to town before becoming blind. A passing motorist found him unconscious and took him to Echuca Hospital, where he had a rough time of it but survived.

According to Belle this was not her husband's closest brush with death. In 1932, the Wades launched their own sideshow and were setting up at Surfers Paradise when Fred received a letter from a collector friend telling him he was forwarding him two death adders. But when the package arrived and Fred had removed two snakes from the straw lining, he was bitten by a third, collected and packed after the letter had been sent. Though antidotes were common and antivenom was just on the market, the Wades relied on ligatures and bleeding. Fred's condition worsened and he was taken to hospital, where he lay, paralysed and blind, for five days before recovering.

Belle herself received a few scratches from fangs but only one proved serious. She was bitten by a tiger snake, and although antivenom was available at the time it was not on hand when she was admitted to hospital. Fortunately, she'd received a non-fatal dose of venom.

In 1939 the Wades broke their partnership, professionally and personally. Belle retired from the snake pits and Fred took on another woman snake handler, whose show name was Jedea.

That Man Gray

Back when the Greenhalghs got into the snake acts, permanent shows in the city proper were another feature of Sydney life. In 1916 a youthful George Cann rented a shop at the railway end of Elizabeth Street and installed a pit. At the other end of the city, on a vacant lot next to the Lowes store, a well-known showman referred to as 'That Man Gray', rented a patch of ground from the council, erected frames, hung his snake pit inside and set up business.

As usual, a legitimate snakey like That Man Gray attracted conmen and charlattans, and in all likelihood one of them was one George Vowels. In February 1917, the *Sydney Morning Herald* reported that a crate of snakes had fallen from a cart in George Street and that one of their captors had been bitten by a venomous snake. Eighteen days later, on 5 March, Vowels, a snake-oil salesman (or antidote vendor) was bitten by a 1-metre tiger snake. He died 23 hours later.

Tests were carried out on the snake and it was stated that both fangs had been damaged (for which read removed) before Vowels was bitten. Removal of fangs is no guarantee, however, that you won't come in contact with the venom if your skin is broken by the stumps.

There were reports at the time that one of Vowels' previous partners, Barnett Alvarez, had died in the same manner about a month before, though his death certificate reveals that he died a full year earlier, on 15 March 1916. 'That Man Gray' was later to die in a mental hospital.

The Millers

The name Miller figures largely in early twentieth-century snake shows. Among them was one John Miller from Queensland. In 1922 he went to Cohuna in Victoria and gave several exhibitions with tiger snakes he had caught on Gunbower Island in the nearby Murray River. One Sunday afternoon he was bitten on the hand during the show. He refused to have it cut by those present and expressed professional confidence in a remedy of his own. It was a full 24 hours before Miller collapsed; he died the following morning.

The famous handler Fred Miller (no relation of John's) worked the pits under the name 'Milo'. He was bred into showbiz; his mother Alice, who worked the snakes as 'Necia' and 'Esmerelda', was possibly the only snake woman to 'accept the bite'. His father was another snake man, and he married a show lass, Amy Ferguson, who also took to the canvas pits.

Another related Miller, Charlie, worked the pits as 'Marco' and 'Marlo', and quite a number of old showies remember him as 'a wild man with a wilder mouth'. Like Milo, he was a good handler, although he had many lucky escapes with bites. A news report of the time tells of Marlo Miller being bitten on the arm and forehead by a tiger snake. He took little notice of it, though the effects soon took hold and he was admitted to Wangaratta Hospital in a serious condition. Both Milo and Marlo had built up resistance through numerous earlier bites, so neither was claimed by snakebite.

Pegleg Davis

In his book *Song of the Snake*, Eric Worrell talks of one 'Pegleg' Davis (also recalled by my pop). Where Davis operated from, and for how long, is lost in the mists of history and failing memories, but it's said that he was in the habit of attaching deadly tiger snakes to his wooden leg . . . until one struck him on his good leg and killed him. It's possible that Pegleg was around just long enough for his name to be recalled, though it must be admitted that the story has the ring of a 'campfire yarn'.

Abdullah and Ram

Nazir Shar began his fairground career running boxing kangaroos and appearing as Abdullah the Indian Mystery Man. But in 1943 he switched to snakes and trained another performer of Indian extraction, Ted Ramsamy. Shar and Ramsamy parted ways in 1945, and Shar moved to the Northern Territory, where he operated a small private zoo in Darwin until his death in 1972.

Ramsamy, however, changed his name to Ram Chandra in 1946 and, billed as the 'Indian Cobra Boy', kept on chasing the crowds. In 1957 he became one of the few people ever to survive a taipan bite, but he was perhaps lucky even to survive to the 1950s.

In 1948, Chandra was booked to perform at the Sydney Easter Show and contacted Pop in his capacity as curator of reptiles at Taronga Park Zoo. Pop filled an order for a number of tiger snakes for Chandra's 'Pit of Death'. It was Chandra's first encounter with tigers and, being unfamiliar with their low, gliding strike, he was bitten on his first show day and was soon in hospital fighting for his life. Antivenom pulled him through, and the following day he was back in the pit, only to be bitten once more. The effects of the second bite were less pronounced, and it seems likely that the serum still in his system was sufficient to counteract the venom.

In 1975, Chandra was awarded the British Empire Medal for his work in collecting taipans and venom for the Commonwealth Serum Laboratories. In many ways he successfully straddled a spectrum of 'snakey' behaviour—from the charlatans and snake-oil salesmen at one end to the collectors, exhibitors and researchers at the other, united in the 'science of show'.

Snake women of renown

And, as I have touched upon here, it wasn't just snake men who drew the crowds, and given that my own mother was one of a long, long line of Cleopatras, I could not fail to acknowledge some of the great snake women of the pits. Some, like Belle Wade, as you have read, were part of teams with their husbands. Others, like Latiefa and Indita, were exotic imported solo performers.

Fred 'Milo' Miller's manager, Captain Gus Leighton, married a show lass, Amy Ferguson, who also took to the canvas pits. Norma 'The Wonder Woman' and Shane 'The Wonder Girl' Brophy, the stepmother and stepsister of Fred Brophy of boxing-tent fame, both served their time in sideshow snake pits.

We first hear of Zillah, the Tasmanian Bush Girl, in a newspaper article from Tasmania reporting how a spate of snake-handler deaths was about to lead to the practice being banned. Readers were advised to see her show at Hobart's Regatta Ground before the plug was pulled: 'It seems rather likely, in consequence of a recent lamentable death, and the fact that during the last 12 months no fewer than nine professional snake charmers have paid a fatal penalty for their temerity, that this type of show was due to be closed down,' said the story.

Zillah was Tasman Bradley's daughter Peggy Goodrick. Tas was my great-uncle and it was he who also got his niece—my mother—into the pits as Cleopatra. Both Peggy and her husband Vic were in showbiz. She worked as a handler for a few years, finally giving the dangerous side of the business away after the Sydney Easter Show of 1920. But the shows were in Peggy's blood, and she and Vic continued their working lives around the circuits and the snake pits. One of their unfortunate handlers, the teenage Jimmy Murray, died when a black tiger snake bit him at Smithton, Tasmania.

Another female snake handler billed as Cleopatra was less fortunate than Zillah. Theresa Caton came from Cunnamulla and was only 27 when her luck ran out at the Manly Beach carnival on 12 March 1920. She was bitten on the finger, not by an asp like her historical namesake but the much deadlier tiger snake, and died the next day. And, as if pursued by fate, both her partners, Anthony Kimbel and Tom Wanless, were to meet similar ends in the following months.

Alf Brydon, his wife and son—all of them snake handlers—travelled to Rockhampton in 1927, where Mrs Brydon was bitten through thick riding breeches just above the knee, and died within twelve hours. She had been demonstrating a previously milked brown snake.

Snake handler Snowy Pink had the pits going strong in the 1920s with Ada, also billed as Miss Kittyhawk, doing the honours, though later she moved into fortune telling . . . Maybe she'd seen her future. Snowy also had an attractive daughter, Thelma, who was only sixteen when she began her career as 'Vonita the Snake Lady'. Venomous snakes were included in her act, and it was almost inevitable that sooner or later she would be bitten. When it happened, however—at the 1928 Lismore Show—the circumstances were unusual. A wild windstorm partly demolished the sideshows, and Thelma was hastily collecting escaped snakes when a red-bellied black—fortunately not the most venomous of snakes—hit her on the hand. She collapsed later and was taken to hospital, where she soon recovered.

In 1922, at the tender age of twelve, Alexie Le Pool got involved in snake shows, working for her father Charles until his death in 1928, then staying with snakes for a further five years.

One of the most attractive of the snake-show performers at this or any other time was Paula Perry. Born Paula Pratt in Lismore in 1912, she became a versatile show performer, starting out on horses at the age of seven and later taking on lion taming, trapeze work and striptease. She married Mick Perry, toured New Zealand, and in 1942 was performing in Manila when the Japanese sweeping through the Philippines overtook her. After more than three years of internment, she went straight back into dancing, performing at Sydney's Celebrity Club.

Aged 35 but looking a good fifteen years younger, she was a *Pix* magazine cover girl in February 1947, and an article in the same issue told of her introduction to snake handling, learning from Pop on his La Perouse pitch. She then diversified even further, working under her own name, as Paulette the Fan Dancer, and in the Pit of Death with both the Wades and Greenhalgh and Jackson.

In 1948 she had a disagreement with Greenhalgh, claiming: 'Arthur wanted me to exaggerate the facts about snakes. I wanted no part of it. He also insisted that I speed up the talks as those present would not move around the boardwalk, and this caused some of the waiting customers to wander off.'

After twelve successful years of tent shows, Paula travelled the world, often receiving top billing in nightclubs as the feathered expressive dancer the 'Ostrich Girl'. In 1973, *Pix* ran an article on the youthful 61-year-old, still a fan dancer and high-kicker, performing with the eighteen-year-olds in an all-girl revue.

The question remains: why did she ever feel she needed to work with venomous snakes? It's not as if she needed to add to her appeal. But then again, Paula never did anything by halves.

*　　*　　*

There are many, many more snakeys than I have recalled here; if you want to read about them too, you'll have to track down a copy of *Snakes Alive*—if you can find one.

APPENDIX

JOHN'S TURTLES

IN MY TIME, I'VE DISCOVERED AND/OR NAMED SEVERAL TURTLES, AS LISTED below. Some of the genus names have now changed but these are the names I gave them.

Discovered and named

Chelodina kuchlingi   Kuchling's turtle, named for Dr Gerald Kuchling.

Elseya irwini   Irwin's turtle, named for Steve Irwin, Queensland.

Elseya georgesi   Georges' turtle, named for Dr (now Professor) Arthur Georges, ACT (now called *Wollumbinia georgesi*).

Elusor macrurus   Mary River turtle, Latin for 'the most elusive', referring to the long hunt for its discovery.

Emydura tanybaraga   Northern yellow-face turtle. Given the local Aboriginal name of a female adult turtle in the Daly River, Northern Territory, by the Ngangi Kurunggurr Group.

Rheodytes leukops   Fitzroy River turtle, Latin for 'white-eyed river diver'.

Six new subspecies

Some of these were well known but undescribed as distinctive, different subspecies for nearly a century. As noted earlier, some scientist don't recognise some of my subspecies, but hundreds of scientists both in Australia and worldwide accept them.

I'm known as a 'splitter' rather than a 'lumper', and it's the lumpers who don't believe in my subspecies. When Professor Legler studied our turtles and first encountered the coastal *Emydura*, he thought they were different enough to be considered full species. In the past, I forwarded to the Australian Museum one of John Legler's letters using the name *Emydura canni* for the Macleay River turtle. John never got around to naming the turtles he intended to, but others, including me, have.

Emydura macquarii dharuk   Sydney Basin turtle, named after Aboriginal people who lived in this region.

Emydura macquarii gunabarra   Hunter River turtle, given the Aboriginal name for the river.

Emydura macquarii dharra   Macleay River turtle, named after the Aboriginal people who named the turtle.

Emydura macquarii binjing   Clarence River turtle, named after the Aboriginal people in the upper reaches of the Clarence River.

Emydura macquarii emmotti   (named with Bill McCord) Emmott's turtle, named after Angus Emmott of Noonbah Station, south-west Queensland.

Emydura macquarii niga   (named with Bill McCord) Fraser Island short-neck turtle, named for its normal black colour.

Rediscovery

Elseya bellii   I rediscovered this species after it was found in an English museum, having been described in 1844. I was informed by photographs sent to me by Anders Rhodin (United States) and historical evidence of where the original came from.

Natural hybrid species

In 1989 I found a dead turtle on the road, in North Queensland Gulf Country, north of the Fitzroy River. This led me to another interesting find which was the meeting point of *C. longicollis* and *C. rankini*—a tremendous blend of all species in shape. Another most interesting form is a hybrid, a long-neck turtle which I collected in North Queensland Gulf country. I was convinced it was a new species. Genetic tests by (then) Dr Arthur Georges of the University of Canberra proved it to be a hybrid between the northern long-neck turtle (*C. longicollis*) and Cann's turtle (*C. rankini*), which saved me the embarrassment of claiming it as a new species. This most fascinating long-neck turtle is a tremendous blend of all species in shape.

These two different genuses of turtle are obviously breeding by themselves at two different locations, and hybridising where they overlap. I've been told by an American expert that for this hybrid turtle to be accepted as a new species, it must be found living and breeding for successive generations in different locations, which has now occurred in a lagoon in the same river system.

ACKNOWLEDGEMENTS

I'D LIKE TO THANK KEITH SMITH, WHOSE TWO VOLUMES OF MEMORIES, PUBLISHED under the title *Johnny Cann: Nature Boy*, provided an inspiring treasury and invaluable road map for this book.

I also thank Ross Sadlier, whose work with me on turtles, especially my photographs, has been outstanding, and Steve Swanson, who rescued and enhanced my ageing pictures.

I want to thank my grand-niece Rachael Cann for helping me turn my thoughts into written words.

And I want to acknowledge the work of Jennie McCulloch, who transcribed hours and hours of interviews without flinching.

Kelly Fagan at Allen & Unwin deserves credit for coming up with this project, and Angela Handley my gratitude for taking it from manuscript to printed book.

And finally, thanks to Jimmy Thomson for weaving all the threads of my life together.

INDEX